D0144931

POSTWAR POLISH POETRY

Czesław Miłosz was born in Lithuania in 1911. A few years later, his father, an engineer, moved the family to Russia, but after World War I he elected to live in Poland, and Miłosz grew up in Wilno, attending Catholic schools there. At college, like many young Poles of his generation, he joined literary-political groups that were influenced by Marxism. He began to write poetry seriously while he was living in Paris, where he came to know his cousin, a French poet, Oscar de L. Milosz. During World War II he worked in Warsaw as writer and editor for the Resistance movement publications. In the first postwar years he was secretary at the Polish Embassy in Washington. In 1951 he left Poland and after ten years in Paris came to the United States where he is now Professor of Slavic Languages and Literatures, Emeritus, at the University of California, Berkeley. In 1980 he was awarded the Nobel Prize for Literature.

Other books by Czesław Miłosz available from the University of California Press are *The History of Polish Literature, Emperor of The Earth* (essays), and *Native Realm* (memoirs).

POSTWAR
POLISH
POETRY

An Anthology
Selected and Edited by

CZESŁAW MIŁOSZ

Third, Expanded Edition

UNIVERSITY OF CALIFORNIA PRESS
Berkeley   Los Angeles   London

University of California Press
Berkeley and Los Angeles, California
University of California Press, Ltd.
London, England

First edition 1965 by Doubleday
Second edition 1970 by Penguin Books
Third edition 1983 by University of California Press
Published by arrangement with Doubleday & Company, Inc.

Library of Congress Cataloging in Publication Data
Main entry under title:

Postwar Polish poetry.

1. Polish poetry—20th century—Translations into
English.   2. English poetry—Translations from Polish.
I. Milosz, Czeslaw.
PG7445.E3P67   1983   891.8'517'08   82-16084
ISBN 0-520-04475-4
ISBN 0-520-04476-2 (pbk.)

The following poems are reproduced here with the kind permission of *Encounter*, London:

"And Even, Even If They Take Away the Stove," "A Ballad of Going Down to the Store," "Self-Portrait as Felt," "Garwolin—a Town for Ever," and "My Jacobean Fatigues," all by Miron Białoszewski and first published in *Encounter*, February 1958. ⓒ 1958 by Encounter Ltd.

"Elegy of Fortinbras," by Zbigniew Herbert and first published in *Encounter*, August 1961. ⓒ 1961 by Encounter Ltd.

"Throughout Our Lands," by Czesław Miłosz and first published in *Encounter*, February 1964. ⓒ 1964 by Encounter Ltd.

The following poems are reproduced here with the kind permission of the *Observer*, London:

"The Return of the Proconsul," "The Tongue," "The Stone," "Mythology," and "The Fathers of a Star," all by Zbigniew Herbert and first published in the *Observer*, September 2, 1962. ⓒ 1962 by the *Observer*, Limited.

All the poems by Witold Gombrowicz, Anna Świrszczyńska, Stanisław Barańczak, and Adam Zagajewski are new to this third edition. The poems "From Songs of a Wanderer" by Aleksander Wat; "A Great Number," "The Joy of Writing," "Utopia," "Autotomy," "Letters of the Dead," "Every Case," and "Laughter" by Wisława Szymborska; and "The Envoy of Mr. Cogito" by Zbigniew Herbert are also new to this edition.

The two monologues from *The Marriage* are from Louis Iribarne's translation of the play, originally published by Grove Press, Inc. (1969) and Calder & Boyars Ltd. (1971); they have been revised by the translator for the present anthology. ⓒ 1969 by Grove Press, Inc., ⓒ 1971 by Calder & Boyars Ltd., ⓒ 1982 by Louis Iribarne.

The translations of the poems from *Building the Barricade*, and the note, "From the Author," were first published in the bilingual edition of *Building the Barricade*, poems of Anna Świrszczyńska translated by Magnus Jan Krynski and Robert A. Maguire (Wydawnictwo Literackie, 1979). Translations ⓒ 1979 by Magnus Jan Krynski and Robert A. Maguire.

The translation of "The Envoy of Mr. Cogito," by Zbigniew Herbert, was first published in *Selected Poems of Zbigniew Herbert*, translated by Bogdana and John Carpenter (Oxford University Press, 1977). ⓒ 1977 by Bogdana and John Carpenter.

The translations of "If You Have to Scream, *Please* Do It Quietly" and "If Porcelain, Then Only the Kind," by Stanisław Barańczak, were first published in *Under My Own Roof*, poems of Stanisław Barańczak translated by Frank Kujawinski (Mr. Cogito Press, 1980). ⓒ 1980 by Mr. Cogito Press.

The translations of "The Humane Conditions," "Never Really," and "Those Men, So Powerful," by Stanisław Barańczak, were first published in *The New York Arts Journal*, no. 23 (1981). ⓒ 1981 by Magnus Jan Krynski and Robert A. Maguire.

The translations of "Freedom," "I Talked to a Frenchman," and "Verses About Poland," by Adam Zagajewski, were first published in *Witness out of Silence: Polish Poets Fighting for Freedom*, translated by Antony Graham (Poets' and Painters' Press, 1980). ⓒ 1980 by Poets' and Painters' Press.

CONTENTS

CONTENTS

CONTENTS

CONTENTS

PREFACE
TO THE THIRD EDITION

THE first edition of this anthology appeared in 1965. It was soon sold out and followed by a second edition, published in England. Subsequently, I was to learn from friends of mine, American poets who in the sixties had been at the outset of their literary careers, that the book had an impact on their work then. It was well received by teachers and students of literature. All this suggests that its reissue, at the initiative of the University of California Press, is justified.

This is an expanded edition. I have added some poems by authors who were already represented and a few by new names. As I said in my first preface, the anthology is not meant to rank the relative merit of authors by allotting them more or less space. Translatability and the editor's whim were more decisive. That whimsical character of the whole is even more pronounced in this edition, and I readily accept the reproach of arbitrariness.

Postwar Polish poetry has gone through several phases marked by changes in the amount of political control. Censorship was relatively tolerant in the years 1945–1949, sterilizing and debasing between 1949 and 1956, then again relaxed but growing unpredictable through the sixties and seventies. The victory of Solidarity in August 1980 opened, for a short time, completely new vistas. The coup of December 1981 closed that chapter; it is too early to predict the future of poetry, which by its nature is a rebellious force.

In expanding the anthology, I translated several

poems especially for the occasion, and I wish to thank my colleague, poet and professor Leonard Nathan, for his assistance in reading and correcting the new material. I decided also to include some English versions done by others and published in separate collections. Thus, all translations are my own unless otherwise noted.

Berkeley, 1982

PREFACE

I WISH to explain in a few words why and how I made this anthology. The underlying motive, as I see it, was my distrust of a poetry which indulges in negation and in a sterile anger at the world. Man confronted with mechanisms beyond his control is a loser until he learns that what seemed to crush him was, in fact, a necessary trial to open a new dimension and to prepare his mind to cope with unheard-of circumstances. This, in my opinion, is what has happened in contemporary Polish poetry. A historical steam-roller has gone several times through a country whose geographical location, between Germany and Russia, is not particularly enviable. Yet the poet emerges perhaps more energetic, better prepared to assume tasks assigned to him by the human condition, than is his Western colleague. One can blame the Polish poet for his irony, sometimes verging on cynicism. Irony, however, for better or worse, is an ingredient of modern poetry everywhere and cannot be separated from the purpose it serves. As for this purpose, elegant scepticism and the will to defend the basic values of man's existence are not one and the same thing.

The anthology is not conceived as an 'image' of contemporary Polish poetry. To make such a claim one would have to allot space to every single poet of talent, a task I found impossible. Some, fine craftsmen, are completely untranslatable, whereas others can be translated without betraying the original. I doubt whether Polish syllabo-tonic verse ('feet' within a line of counted syllables) can be rendered in English. Consequently, there is in my book a distortion of perspective, as poets who use the traditional metre could hardly be included. It is true, however, that in the last decades they have been less and less numerous; the younger generation tends to practise a kind of asceticism or 'anti-poetry'; thus the fluidity of rocking rhythms and rhymes is usually abandoned. Generally speaking, adaptability to English determined to a large extent the number of poems each writer has been allotted.

I limited the scope of the anthology to poets who are living, with one exception. The stress is laid upon poems published since 1956, a date when the lifting of censorship and the breakdown of absurd doctrines provoked a real explosion of new schools and talents. Here, of course, I make several exceptions, going back sometimes as far as the years of World War II or the years preceding it. Poems were judged on merit alone and I did not apply any discrimination as to the views of their authors or their political status. Neither did I examine their passports; no clear-cut division between the poets living abroad and those at home is apparent in Polish literature, in contrast to what occurred in Russian literature. Since Polish poets have been influencing each other across the borders, their present residence is not a decisive factor.

A reader could be puzzled, I would imagine, by the character of this poetry and be curious about its literary kinships. Its mixture of macabre and humorous elements, its preoccupation less with the ego than with dramas of history, the relish with which it handles and remodels moral maxims did not appear all of a sudden in our time; several centuries of native verse, baroque perhaps by the very nature of the language, are behind it. Italian and

French influences, to mention the most significant in the past, were modified accordingly. And as every poetic current is embedded in local traditions even if it absorbs a great deal from abroad, the pattern has been repeated up to this day. Rebellious French writers have exerted a strong influence since the end of the nineteenth century when the first translations of Arthur Rimbaud were published. Yet the work of one patron and martyr of modern Polish verse, Cyprian Norwid (1821–83), has been leading poets in a direction opposite to that of the French. Norwid, slighted and rejected in his lifetime, was a poet of anthropological structures; he confronted the industrial era with the Mediterranean civilizations of the past; the ironic wisdom of that downtrodden man, an emigré in Italy, in New York, in Paris, overcame subjectivism. Today Polish poetry is the result of a distillation of themes and forms, conducted by successive vanguards. Great conciseness is often achieved, and very short poems contain intricate meanings. I must admit I am partial to a poetry that sometimes attains the calligraphic quality of an ideogram. To my surprise I discovered it translates better than long poems, as if the reduction of images and metaphors to a bare minimum made it more universal and less inclined to be trapped in a linguistic laboratory.

Poets of each country resemble an eighteenth-century freemasonic lodge, with its rites, rivalries and friendships. Being a member of such a lodge myself, I am glad to act as its representative abroad. The majority of the authors in the anthology are younger than myself and to introduce them is particularly pleasant. I hope my fellow poets will not hold a grudge against me for not giving some of them a more prominent place. Translations should at least be adequate, and it is better not to attempt what cannot be done.

I am not a native English speaker and I do not trust my ear, so I had to rely upon the help and control of those who have spoken English from childhood; poetry, after all, always draws upon the language of one's childhood. I wish to thank Mac Goodman, Lawrence Davis, Reuel Wilson, and Richard Lourie for the long debates we had over one sentence or, quite often, over one word. Two poems of Slonimski and one of Jastrun ('Remembrance') were given definitive shape by Lawrence Davis. Some poems were translated by Peter Dale Scott with my minor assistance and are marked accordingly.

1965

LEOPOLD STAFF

(1878–1957)

STAFF'S name is usually associated with the 'Young Poland' movement which prior to World War I revolutionized Polish poetry. After that time, he accompanied several generations of poets, teaching them craft, but even more learning from them and constantly changing his technique. A man of broad humanist education, he directed before 1914 an excellent series, 'Symposium', for one of the publishing houses, in which, among other authors, Nietzsche, Kierkegaard and Cardinal Newman appeared. An amusing detail indicative of the syncretic mood of the period is that he himself simultaneously translated Nietzsche and the *Flowers* of Saint Francis. His translations from Latin, Italian, French and German, both in verse and in prose, are a durable achievement. I used to visit him during the last war in Nazi-occupied Warsaw. A gentle old man with a goatee, he was venerated by much younger poets for his passionate interest in their work, his optimism – very necessary at that time – and the poems he sent to underground publications. After 1945 Staff profited considerably from his friendships with very young poets, then entering the literary scene, and, being open to their judgements, attained his long-sought ideal: complete simplicity of form. The poems which follow belong to his last phase. Though he is no longer living, there is no doubt as to his place among the poets of today.

LEOPOLD STAFF

Foundations

I BUILT on the sand
And it tumbled down,
I built on a rock
And it tumbled down.
Now when I build, I shall begin
With the smoke from the chimney.

The Bridge

I DIDN'T believe,
Standing on the bank of a river
Which was wide and swift,
That I would cross that bridge
Plaited from thin, fragile reeds
Fastened with bast.
I walked delicately as a butterfly
And heavily as an elephant,
I walked surely as a dancer
And wavered like a blind man.
I didn't believe that I would cross that bridge,
And now that I am standing on the other side,
I don't believe I crossed it.

Three Towns

THREE small towns,
So small that all of them
Could be contained in one . . .

2

They are not on the map.
They were destroyed in the war,
For in them lived people
Who were hard-working, quiet,
Peace-loving.

O tepid, indifferent brothers!
Why does none of you look for those towns?
How poor is the man who
Asks no questions.

ANTONI SŁONIMSKI
(1895–1976)

IN 1918 a group of poets founded a literary café in Warsaw, 'Under the Picadore', where they used to read their poems to the public. Soon they started to publish a poetry magazine, *Skamander*, named, in a reference to the *Iliad*, after the river on which Troy had stood. Although they were very different from each other in their temperaments and aspirations, they have been known since under the group name. They were bound by a common desire to renew the poetic language and to achieve perfection within the framework of traditional metrics. Słonimski, one of the leaders, came from a Warsaw family of scientists and scholars. He may be called a poet of the Warsaw liberal intelligentsia, attuned to their taste for debating world problems and their lyrico-sarcastic attitudes. His range in poetry extends from pure lyricism to a sly mockery; his plays, feuilletons, and parables in prose have been satirical weapons used by him in numerous encounters. A rationalist, a pacifist, much in the spirit of H. G. Wells, he expressed in the nineteen thirties the despair of the liberals threatened as they were by the rise of National Socialism in neighbouring Germany and by chauvinist, anti-semitic Rightists in Poland, while to the east Stalinist Russia did not give much reason for hope. After Hitler crushed Poland, Słonimski succeeded in escaping abroad and for many years lived in England. He returned to Poland around 1950 and lived somewhat in the shade until he came to the fore in 1956 as one of the most active spokesmen of the intellectuals opposing totalitarian controls. *Skamander* poets are not readily translated. Słonimski, for instance, loses in translation the interesting contrast between the songlike, slightly melancholy fluidity of his rhymed lines and the logic of his discourse – which is a formal allusion to his Romantic predecessors.

Hamletism

LONG did I look into the dark eyes of my brother,
Into eyes well-known, although the face was not,
As he spoke, as he cautiously weighed out each word
In Leningrad, on sombre Marat Street.

Michal, Aunt Fanny's, Uncle Ludwik's son,
Names which awake the wistful taste of childhood,
Sternly and gravely concludes the discussion.
And yet he's my cousin. A very close relation.

Magnitogorsk and Urals. With us or against.
Stalin, the Party. Vast, incessant toil.
The Five-Year Plan. As children five years old
We used to exchange letters. Michal looks ill.

Light of young eyes, yet hair untimely grey.
Calm, but intent, faithful in what you do,
You serve and you want to serve your country well
And you say: 'Good night, prince.' – 'Good night,
    Horatio.'

1933
Translated by Peter Dale Scott
and Czesław Miłosz

To the Germans

PROUDLY looking at the ruins of the conquered city,
Carrying a short, bloody sword, from an empty yard
A Roman barbarian entered the house of Archimedes
When the legion of Marcellus conquered Syracuse.

Half-naked, breathing heavily, in his dusty helmet,
He stopped, his nostrils drinking in new blood and
    crime.
'Noli tangere circulos meos' –
Said Archimedes gently, drawing in the sand.

On the circle, along the diameter and the inscribed
    triangle
The blood ran in a dark and living sign.
Archimedes, defend yourself against the mercenary!
Archimedes, who are murdered today!

Your blood sank into the sand, but your spirit lives.
Not true. The spirit dies as well. Where do traces
    remain?
In the marble of your house are adders' nests.
The wind spins circles out of sand on ruined Hellas.

1937

Defence of the Moon

THE friend of lovers, the poets' companion
Has faithfully brightened the night for centuries.
It is with you who love, with you who dream,
Who should defend the moon if not poets?

Let it swim in silver sleep. Is Earth not sufficient
For the eternal task of Sisyphus and Antigone's despair?
Must we also have that target, that superearthly shield,
Which turns the sky into a firing range?

Gluttonous eater of animal corpses, lewd
Murderer and destroyer, fertile beyond measure,
Motivated by Nature's two imperatives:
To save one's own hide and to propagate the species,

He grows already, he arms himself, an astral hero.
The Mare Imbrium, the quiet Mare Tenebrarum,
The Valley of Herodotus and Tycho's Crater
He will fill with human agony and the nightmare of
    Earth.

Moral law is in me and the starry sky
Is above me. So what, if Law is disgraced by Oppression?
Let the moons turn unchanged in their courses,
Let at least the sky remain pure.

JAROSŁAW IWASZKIEWICZ
(1894–1979)

ANOTHER poet of *Skamander*, Iwaszkiewicz bears little resemblance to Słonimski. Born in the Ukraine and brought up in Kiev, where he studied music at the conservatory, he remained for a long time after he migrated to Warsaw an exotic newcomer. His early poetry and stylized prose showed the impact of his Ukrainian childhood and adolescence. Lavish colours, hieratical Byzantine shapes were among the ingredients of his fancy aestheticism seasoned with all sorts of foreign influences. If the poets of *Skamander*, with the obvious exception of Słonimski, worshipped Life as a primeval force wiser than the intellect (they were, in fact, poets of the irrational 'élan vital'), Iwaszkiewicz pushed that tendency to an extreme. He travelled much all over Europe, served for a while as a diplomat in Copenhagen and Brussels, and puzzled literary critics by the amoral, Dionysiac and, at the same time, pessimistic character of his work. The younger generation reproached him for a complete indifference to social and political causes, yet they were attracted to his demoniac art. During World War II, Iwaszkiewicz was the only *Skamander* poet who remained in Poland, and his home near Warsaw was a periodic meeting place for many writers and artists engaged in the resistance movement. After the war he was for many years the editor of an excellent literary monthly, *Twórczość* (*Creative Work*). His own work embraces poetry, short stories, novels, plays, translations and articles on music. In his poetry he combines a fondness for conventions borrowed from past epochs (the madrigal, the letter in verse, the ode) with a subjective, capricious metaphysics of sensuality. The most controversial of the *Skamander* group, he always had many detractors and admirers.

Quentin Matsys

THE adolescent Christ closes with his fingers
The dying eyes of his grandmother Anne.
And his chin trembles. Saint Joachim
Passes into his hands a wax candle.
The violet of Polish mists, of Florentine hills
Is set in Flemish folds; green fringes
Are thrust upon our eyes like proclamations
Of truth. These mark the boundaries for silks:
Sky and light. All this is traversed
By a hot stream; so, let us turn away
Our red-haired heads and try to untangle
The silky locks, the pearly braids
Of Mary Magdalen; and look at fragrance
Ground to a paste of white grease
And lifted up in a golden box
By a translucent palm.
                              If there is a limit
Between heaven and earth and if angels
Smaller than men and lighter – green, similar
To giant locusts – dance more joyous dances
And eat fruits dripping with a sweeter juice
Upon crimson paintings – then there is in the world
No visible difference between the tremors
Of death and the gold of blue landscapes.
The angel and Anne on the verdigris plain
Take flight, more real than my heart
And sharper than the pain that is wounding
My legs, pierced by a javelin, my hands lacerated
And stained with the blood of a mystical scorn.
No, no, really, there is something after all:

Green and gold, witnesses of angels;
And Joachims, with their eyes fixed on high,
Feel that from the silks of iridescent garments
Half malachite, half raspberry rose
The true life results. Is it eternal?
I don't know, we don't know, they don't know. Black
    Satans
Have fallen into the bronze of frames, the corners of
    triptychs.
They keep in their hands what I am: man.
And other people mean to me as much
As those Satans in their attire of coppery
Scales. Hosanna! Hosanna!
Let the adolescent Christ close our eyes;
Like Anne the saint we will die without knowing
The limits of the world.

1937

KAZIMIERZ WIERZYŃSKI
(1894-1969)

A NATIVE of the Carpathian mountain region, a soldier in the Austrian army in World War I, and prisoner of war in Russia, later one of the founders of *Skamander*, Wierzyński acquired fame by early poems full of adolescent exuberance and joy of life. In the nineteen twenties he was one of the first European poets to glorify athletics and his volume *The Olympic Laurel* won first prize for a literary work honouring sport at the Olympic Games of 1928. His dithyrambic poetry becomes tragic in tone after 1930, reproducing the all-European pattern of the impasse. This is also true of other *Skamander* poets, particularly of Julian Tuwim (1894-1953), whose violent political diatribes of rare linguistic force I find untranslatable. After the defeat of Poland by the Nazis, Wierzyński went into exile and after 1940 he lived in the United States. His poetry written in America went through several stages. In the war years it reverted to the patriotic motives of Polish romanticism. Afterwards, his almost desperate struggle with isolation found its expression in natural imagery drawn from the East Coast. He remained a poet of youthful enthusiasm, in revolt against his own despair and the inhumanity of his century. After 1956, a date which marks a revival in Polish letters, he drew closer in his style to young poets publishing in Poland. The poems of his last decade are striking in their generosity and openness to the world. They probably rank among his highest accomplishments.

A Word to Orphists

WHO is standing behind me I don't know, but I know
    he is there,
What he is saying I don't know, but I repeat after him,
I don't hear the words, but I am able to write them down
And this is so important that I ask no questions.

There was a time when I looked backward,
I wanted to see into his eyes,
But he vanished before I could grasp his shape.
Then I moved about confounded and since he would
    not appear
I dried into dust, I faded
Into an absurdity, colourless and human.

In the morning I would sit at my desk and hold a pencil,
I knew what I wanted to write and felt I could not do it,
I waited till night as it is easier for him to come in the
    dark,
To stop behind me and, unseen, whisper.

But no, he would not come. I would take a forgotten
    manuscript
And read aloud those words from behind my shoulder,
    from beyond me,
I would ask: how did it all come to me?
And I called out: after all this is from you,
Respond, you who are inscrutable.
No more shall I look backward.

Then I understood the true fate of Orpheus,
That love is a constant terror of loss.
So I call to you, Orphists, if any of you will trust me,
Repeat the whispered words you hear,
Do not look to see who stands behind you.
It is good, it is marvellous that he exists.

ALEKSANDER WAT

(1900–1967)

AROUND 1919 Wat and his friends made much noise in Warsaw by their futurist (rather dadaist) manifestoes calling for a conscious debasement of the language and ridiculing the harmonious verse of *Skamander*. This revolt against ordered speech proved short-lived, and the trend was not to be revived until much later. Wat, after his first anarcho-mystical writings, was for many years active in literary criticism and editing. His sarcastic tales of anticipation, *The Unemployed Lucifer*, foreshadowed his later poetry. In 1929–32 he edited an important leftist periodical, *The Literary Monthly*. In 1939, fleeing the Nazis, he found himself in the area taken over by Soviet troops, was arrested, accused of hostility towards the authorities, and spent some six years as a prisoner and a deportee in Russia. After his return to Poland he resumed his literary activities, but in the period of the 'frost' between 1949 and 1956 he remained in limbo because of his unorthodox views and earned his living by doing translations. His poems published in 1956 after a long compulsory silence were greeted by the young generation as an important event in Polish letters. Wat's later poetry, with its intentional inconsistencies and buffooneries, its philosophical seriousness, its fusion of personal and historical elements, was certainly very far from the genteel and the tamed, those scapegoats of the young. For a literary critic it is a curious example of belated fulfilment, and at the same time of a once-defeated movement taking its revenge: dadaist and surrealist gropings in the twenties (hidden under the name of futurism) had against them both *Skamander* and the rationalistic, constructivist First Vanguard. After 1959, when he went to the South of France because of his health, Wat lived abroad. His Mediterranean poems are among his best. He died in Paris.

Before Breughel the Elder

WORK is a blessing.
I tell you that, I – professional sluggard!
Who slobbered in so many prisons! Fourteen!
And in so many hospitals! Ten! And innumerable inns!
Work is a blessing.
How else could we deal with the lava of fratricidal love
    towards fellow men?
With those storms of extermination of all by all?
With brutality, bottomless and measureless?
With the black and white era which does not want to
    end
endlessly repeating itself da capo like a record
forgotten on a turntable
spinning by itself?
Or perhaps someone invisible watches over the phono-
    graph? Horror!
How, if not for work, could we live in the paradise of
    social hygienists
who never soak their hands in blood without aseptic
    gloves?
Horror!
How else could we cope with death?
That Siamese sister of life
who grows together with it – in us, and is extinguished
    with it
and surely for that reason is ineffective.
And so we have to live without end,
without end. Horror!
How, if not for work, could we cope with ineffective
    death

(Do not scoff!)
which is like a sea,
where everyone is an Icarus, one of nearly three billion,
while besides, so many things happen
and everything is equally unimportant, precisely,
    unimportant
although so difficult, so inhumanly difficult, so painful!
How then could we cope with all that?
Work is our rescue.
I tell you that – I, Breughel, the Elder (and I, for one,
your modest servant, Wat, Aleksander) – work is our
    rescue.

To Be a Mouse

To be a mouse. Preferably a field mouse. Or a garden
    mouse –
but not the kind that live in houses.
Man exhales an abominable smell!
We all know it – birds, crabs, rats.
He provokes disgust and fear.
    Trembling.

To feed on wisteria flowers, on the bark of palm trees,
to dig up roots in cold, humid soil
and to dance after a fresh night. To look at the full moon,
to reflect in one's eyes the sleek light of lunar
    Agony.

To burrow in a mouse hole for the time when wicked
    Boreas
will search for me with his cold, bony fingers
in order to squeeze my little heart under the blade of his
    claw
a cowardly mouse heart –
    A palpitating crystal.

From Persian Parables

By a great, swift water
on a stony bank
a human skull was lying
and shouting: Allah la ilah.

And in that cry such horror
and such supplication
so great was its despair
that I asked the helmsman:

For what can it still cry out? Of what is it still afraid?
What divine judgement could strike it yet again?

Suddenly there came a wave
took hold of the skull
and tossing it about
smashed it against the bank.

Nothing is ultimate
– the helmsman's voice was hollow –
and there is no bottom to evil.

A Flamingo's Dream

WATER water water. And nothing but water.
If only an inch of land! An inch of no-matter-what land!
To set one foot on! If only!

We begged the gods for that! All of them!
Water gods, land gods, southern gods, northern gods,
For an inch, a strip, a scrap of any kind of land!
No more than just to support a claw of one foot!
And nothing. Only water. Nothing except water.
Water water water.
If only a speck of land!
There is no salvation.

From 'Notes Written in Obory'

X WAS asked
            if he believed in the objective existence of
                        Parzota.
– To believe in the objective existence of Parzota –
                        that smacks of mysticism,
I am an old horse, you know, and a staunch
rationalist
answered X.
The sequel was more interesting.

X persisted in his refusal to believe in the objective
    existence of Parzota
Who, the said Parzota, placed him in a dungeon, put him
    to torture.

21

Yet everything would have been in perfect order
if not for one sad circumstance:
the stupid man of principle was so obstinate that he died
    in the dungeon.
Poor Parzota! Condemned to eternal doubt.
Now he will never find out
if he existed objectively.

Arithmetic

WHEN you are alone
don't think you are alone.
He (she) is always with you.

Anywhere you go
you are always followed.
The most faithful dog is not so faithful,
a shadow sometimes disappears,
he (she) – never.

That red-haired whore is leaning against the doorway
    of a hotel
and with her is – not her double – she, another she.
That old man sneaks in after her like a cat
and with him is his inseparable companion.

Those two on a bed in contortions.
These two sit at the foot and wait, sadly hanging their
    heads.

If the Word 'Exists'

IF the word 'exists' is to have any meaning
it should refer to something to which we can return.
Yet there is no return! Everything is once
and before it has begun to 'exist', it has already ceased to
   'exist'.
(Notice 'has begun' and 'has ceased' are equally un-
founded) and the alternation 'is' and 'is not' is not a
sequence of time, it unfolds itself beyond time – in so
far as 'unfolds'
can be used here.
Therefore
let us turn again to essence. For with it we are more
   certain.
Since we create it ourselves. It is not dependent
either upon whether it 'is', or whether it 'is not'.

How good it is to return to old rejected concepts!
(N.B. The meaning of that 'let us return' is common. So,
   for example, Odysseus returned to Penelope, to
   her who knew the secret:
that one must weave and unweave. And again weave and
   unweave.)

Notes to the Books of the
Old Testament

I Kings, 10   *To K. Jeleński*

ON the eastern sidewalk of Magdalen College a small
turtle reflected a long time before he answered

my question, he moved his jaws like a meccano:
                                             'That
even I cannot remember: I am hardly
two hundred and ninety-three. But in our family
a record has been preserved how our ancestor, of blessed
        memory,
assisted at the loves of the queen of Sheba with your
        great-grandfather.
As to the riddles she presumably asked him to solve, our
        tradition
is silent. What is known: it occurred in a wine-coloured
        chamber where instead of lamps gold was shining,
        from Tyre, no doubt. My ancestor, was not a learned
        turtle, though a respectable one, for certain. . . .'
With short steps we shuffled after him, I, my beautiful
wife and Adriana, our charming guide.
We listened to the turtle solemnly. When he lost his
        breath
my wife with a kind stroke of her finger
animated his little snout. After all, that's why I wander!
In strange lands! In my old age!
I write, that is to say, my autobiography and gather data
for the genealogy of our ancient stock. An English duke
brought the turtle to my attention, in a waterfront dive
        in Naples
in return for a bowl of spaghetti and a glass
of wine ('My great-great-grandfather, an admiral,
took that turtle to Oxford all the way from Abyssinia').
Thus all three of us we listened to the turtle with the
        solemnity due
to a dignified university person. This time
the pause was irritatingly long when all of a sudden,

from behind an island, young laughter was heard
and a boat passed, carrying a couple away.
Neither of them graceful. But my wife was delighted
to hear laughter of lovers. There is no need to add
that tiptoeing after the turtle and straining to hear
what he might deign to tell us, we were bent so low
that one may say we were on all fours.
Were they laughing at this? At their love?
At love in general? It does not matter.
                                        'So, hardly had
he turned over on his back when he asked: "And now
tell me, baby, what do they think of me in your country?"
The queen, still in rapture: "That you love wisdom,"
she faltered, "and women." "Wisdom?" he replied,
    "I don't deny.
But women? Hardly. I love femininity."'

Again there was a pause. This time not laughter but
    crying
and that of an infant, indeed, more bizarre here
than for instance a drunkard's railing in a cathedral.
                                        'And he was right,'
the turtle added at last. 'He was wrong!' exclaimed
charming Adriana, blushing all over. She never inter-
    rupted
her elders, since she was a true young lady. 'He was
right,'
the turtle repeated, as though he had not heard. 'A great
    lord
should love only universals: grassiness but not grass,
not humans but humanity, and arsiness but not . . .'
                                        Whether he finished or not

I don't know, for Adriana again interjected, it is true,
    somewhat
abashed: 'He who never loved someone, knows no love
at all.' The turtle fell silent, for good; now he had taken
offence: nobody here had dared to contradict him.
We had no flies or anything else to smooth over the
    incident.
But my wife, who has a way with animals
and children, gently massaged his jowls.
So he spoke again, this time even garrulous:

'When king Solomon rolled off the queen for the third
    time,
he asked: "Now, what counsel do your people ask for?
What do they want from me?" "A toenail", answered
the queen of Sheba, "from the little toe of your foot."
"I'll give it to them," agreed the king and himself
handed her a pair of nail scissors. She pulled out a
    golden cup
artfully engraved by the hand of Hiram-Abi
which the king after their first intercourse had presented
    to her,
with a tight lid, upon it was carved the grim face of
    Ashtoreth.
A short cry, blood spurted into the cup, the lid slams. . . .
What happened next, our ancestor did not relate.
Perhaps the whole thing so tired him, the strain upon his
    eyes,
upon his attention, that he suddenly fell asleep.
He was not learned. Who, after all, in those times
was learned?'
               'But what happened to the cup?

The cup?' I asked hollowly. For just then
a thought disturbed me, that perhaps
if I drink the blood of my ancestor
youth, eternal, wisdom, for ever, will be restored to me!
                    'Oh yes,' the turtle replied impassively,
'we know. The ship carrying the queen back, sank.
    Thirteen centuries later Senegalese sailors extracted
    the cup
from the belly of a whale, on the Indian ocean.' 'Un-
    damaged?'
'Undamaged.' Again a pause. 'From Abyssinia, an
    Italian airman stole it together with the treasure of
    the King of Kings
    not long ago. . . . His plane fell into Etna.'
'Into Etna!' I cried in falsetto, I straightened up
as well as I could and I raised my arms into the air,
frightening by this motion two male cardinals
that were fighting a knightly battle
on the grass, plucking at each other's beautiful scarlet
    crests.
                'And yet Etna threw back the cup,'
unexpectedly screeched the turtle. 'Like a sandal?' 'Of
    Empedocles,'
he asserted with a vivid satisfaction. Again silence. The
    crying of the infant had long subsided. And the
    laugh of the lovers. And the hisses of the birds. I
    could not stand this pause.
'Where is the blood of my ancestor?' I shouted, full of
    hope.
                'Blood, blood, blood,'
he grated angrily. Adriana got up: 'I wanted, master,
to sit at your feet and imbibe words of wisdom from your

lips. And now . . .' she sobbed, poor, dear Adriana.
    'Blood,
of blood, with blood,' repeated the turtle, obviously
    unable to stop. 'You gulped the blood of my cousins,
    is not that enough? Seizing them in whole fistfuls in
    the bulrushes by the river Ili, crushing and smashing
    them with a rolling pin, on the rough table in the
    kitchen of the Prokombinat where you helped the
    dirty woman cook to steal food. The blood of my
    brothers splashed into your eyes, bespattered your
    face, your rags, you waded in their blood, still you
    had not enough. You have never had enough. Not
    enough. Not enough . . .'

I was afraid that he would have a stroke, he was choking.
Ashamed, we fled across the lawns and for a long time
the gargoyles of Magdalen pursued us with their howling
    laughter.

From 'Songs of a Wanderer'

Ich stech das Licht. Ich stech das Licht
Ich stech das Hertz das ich liebe
    Schönwerth. *Aus der Oberplatz:*
    Sitten und Sagen

II

DISGUSTED by everything alive I withdrew into the
    stone world: here
I thought, liberated, I would observe from above, but
    without pride, those things

entangled in chaos. With the eyes of a stone, myself
　　　　　a stone among stones,
　　　　　and like them sensitive,
pulsating to the turning of the sun. Retreating into
　　　　　the depth of myself-stone,
motionless, silent; growing cold; present through a
　　　　　waning of presence—in the cold
attractions of the moon. Like sand diminishing in
　　　　　an hour-glass, evenly,
Ceaselessly, uniformly, grain by grain. Thus I shall be
　　　　　submitted
only to the rhythms of day and night. But—
no dance in them, no whirling, no frenzy: only
　　　　　monastic rule, and silence.
They do not become, they are. Nothing else. Nothing
　　　　　else, I thought, loathing
all which becomes.
　　　　　　　I, a stone among stones. O, never had I thought
of stone in the words of death. I had always felt in it
　　　　　a heart, a pulsation
of its life, and not just in its internal structures,
　　　　　which amaze
onlookers, photographers, mineralogists. . . . Simply:
　　　　　the heart of a stone: Simply:
the dreams of a stone. To be in the heart of a stone—
　　　　　how much I desired this!
In the heart of a stone, without the flaw which
　　　　　through our tainted veins
slushes deep into our hearts and grows, making them
　　　　　totally putrid matter,
subjected to all decay.

The dreams of a stone! how I wanted
                to see the dreams
of a stone, through its own stony eyes! Perhaps
                a human child, an infant.
when it is no longer a palpitating sponge of flesh,
                but not yet—a man,
perhaps, in his eye, he retains a dream of a stone,
                not even a dream—
a reflection, an echo of a dream, distant and
                fading away. O,
how I wanted to be in the thought of a stone, to be what
                its thought thinks. Or—
cursed in the beginning, exiled from stone, how I
                wanted to touch
the thought of a stone, just as I touch rose petals,
                careful not to let it feel
my coarse, bulbous fingers, the fingers of a usurper:
it might die of disgust.
                The thought of a stone, the thought of a rose,
                what if they were akin?
in its very short season, when it is still folded-up wisdom,
and yet open to love; Eros, agapè—as I call this
                in the obscure speech
of men, in speech without eyes, no—with eyes
                repeatedly gouged out;
in snail words sent in whispers toward our cannibal lips
by our brain, which is nourished with blood,
                subjected to rottenness, decay, putridity,
contaminating everything in its grasp with putridity,
                decay. What's erosion, I thought,
to a stone? What's the crumbling of its inner structures?
                The heart of a stone

is not in structures, in time-space relations? it is generous
rebuilding structures, while time, impotent, disintegrates
           them. The heart of a stone
does not submit to annihilation, to the death of
           everything which becomes.
                         Armored,
it is a sovereign monad.
           I didn't envy the stone the riches of
           its inner world.
I did not look for a shell to hide in, to gorge my mollusk
           senses on the food of colors.
What are riches to the stone? Yes, in riches we surpassed
stones during our million-years' existence on earth. But
           what are riches to them?
In their inner world nothing but poverty—as we call it,
           using the gouged-out eyes
of our poor speech. But everything there is meaningful
           and pure, everything there is everything.
Only there. If God exists, he is there. At the heart
           of stones. Also—in their dreams.
           Even the tree, the most perfect creation
           of the demiurge
just before he fell asleep, when he was dozing on the
           same edge above which
nods the head of a schoolboy, tired from poring over
           a book on the table,
on that edge from which something irresistibly pulls us
           down, into the dark,
           down and into the dark
from where we rose and rise obstinately—even the tree,
           I repeat,

when, like a strong man, it wedges into the stone
                    and splits it apart
with its savage, dirt-covered, worm-coated root;
                    when it pulls out of mother earth
and without shame brings to light her magic dreams:
                    leaves, birds, grains,
even the tree, always prepared for flights, vibration,
                    frenzy—even the tree—
I repeat, the most beautiful creation of the demiurge
                    while on the edge of sleep—
what can it do to the stone?
                    Perhaps, in the instant of his vertigo,
the wildest creature, in whom was set the terrifying
                    spark of genius,
so desiring to die out! so unhappy is it in that dwelling-
                    place—perhaps man in vertigo
has a flash of intuition, when he approaches stones
                    with pain, yet without noise,
                    without pride?
a sculptor whose chisel, already lifted, is held back
                    by the voice of the stone:
stop, here is your threshold, one scratch more and you
                    will be rejected inexorably,
without return.
                    So I thought about stone. And
                    since I loved everything
that is not even the negation of stone—but worse:
                    otherness, all,
that is subjected to flaws, transience, death and—
                    worse: resurrection

from death; and since I was sensuous to the marrow
        of my marrow,
since I loved my senses, my skin, all skin, every skin
        even unto
fiery hatred—the heart of a stone was closed to me,
sealed fast.
        But now is the time of old age. Aetas
        serenitatis. Thus, disgusted
with the world of the living, its beauty turned toward
        death, decaying, rising
from the dead as vermin, as acrid weeds, as manure
        for peasant hands, thus
I fled into the stone world, in order—a stone among
        stones, done with pride,
although from above—to slowly close my eyes, not yet
        stony but no longer human,
to your sufferings, to your tenderness, to your labors
        and those agonies
of yours, to all that is subjected to incessant putrefaction,
that is our torture, our shame, our shameful pity,
our beauty like radiant eyes in the face of a
        hydrocephalic hunchback.

III

So now, having fled into the stone world, I was slowly
        falling asleep, a stone under
my head, feeling how the warmth of its heart penetrates
        my head,
and makes it similar, its twin; when on the edge
        of sleep, from where,
heavy with darkness we lean into greater darkness—
        now, when I dream there: I, too,

am a stone among stones, and, like them, I am exalted
                    yet without pride, inert
and yet tense with strength, in a tense fullness which
                    hangs in the clenched stone fist
of the moon over a sterile landscape—
          I was awakened by the din of those
whom I survived.
                    Remember! Remember!
     Not in a double row did they surround me;
                    not in the carriage
of a survivor must I pass them; no holiday dresses
                    do they wear:
no wreaths on their heads. Naked, though tightly
                    swathed in the lava
of clay. Like that one in Pompeii, who just managed
                    to lower his brow
lifted in amazement and to fix his tired death-stare
                    on the earth
which betrayed him.
               Remember! Remember!—They shout:
                    and they want to be forgotten.
Remember!—They shout: and they want eternal
                    oblivion. Our hell—
is in the memory of those who will survive us.
          Driven out by the din and the sham
of those whom I survived, I walked down through
                    rubble. And having lost
everything I knew in that difficult descent, I am
                    again that
which I had been.

JULIAN PRZYBOŚ

(1901–1970)

POLISH poetry in the years 1918–39 was marked by battles be-
tween *Skamander* and the Vanguard, which, in turn, is usually
divided into the First and the Second. In the 1920s Przyboś,
theoretician of poetry as well as poet, directed the First Van-
guard's forays against its enemies, from its stronghold in the me-
dieval city of Cracow. He came from a poor peasant family in
southern Poland, and his native village is always alive in his
poetry, making a curious contrast with his socialist cult of techno-
logy. Through his clinging to principles he gave to the Vanguard
schools an orientation opposed to that of French dadaism and
surrealism. He saw in a poem a nearly mathematical construction
of metaphors, and he condemned the *Skamander* poets for their
obedience to an uncontrollable demon, for the melody in their
verse, and for their autobiographical lyricism. He elaborated a
system of prescriptions: the poet should use the least number of
words possible and, avoiding direct expression of his feelings,
create their emotional equivalents in his images; he should not be
carried away by rhythmical incantation. As a result of this pro-
gramme, the First Vanguard abandoned traditional metres and
was accused of writing no more than a dense, metaphorical prose.
Przyboś, a teacher of literature before the war, returned at the
time of the Nazi occupation to his native village and wrote
resistance poems which were circulated clandestinely. After the
war he served for several years as the Minister of the Polish
People's Republic to Switzerland. He is the author of many
studies on the history of Polish literature. In his poetic practice
his obsession with a poetry controlled by the will sometimes
leads him to the very edge of the ridiculous, but he is recognized
as one of those who contributed most to the transformations of
modern Polish verse.

JULIAN PRZYBOŚ

Mother

HE dreamed of overturned Gothic cathedrals
attacking like drills unconquerable capitals, of
buildings which when circled by a car would move
off in the streets, of windows on high thrown up
along a hundred floors of the air, hoops growing
rounder and rounder,
of a man-bird with a cloud instead of a parachute,
   preceded by cyclists pedalling colourful sign-
   boards,
of sudden cataracts of roofs, the clenching of a fist
   squeezing countries into stone sceptres and golden
   hammers,
of weeping auroras, of spurting fires –
Before him stood his mother, a thousand immobile
   kilometres, covered with distance as with the bark
   of a roadside willow
and the roosters of two contradictory villages crowed
   noon and evening at once,
while
on the crossroads signposts trembled with each
   movement of his hand, jumping back and forth as
   in a compass shaken
and the thick earth, heavy with the dead, resisted the
   thrusts of his heart.

1937

36

On the Shore

ON the mirror two naked boys wearing enormous fins
  snorted thin streamlets through noses and mouths,
in the midst of the waters they were blowing up an
  immense glass chalice or a key,
seizing a falling oar they stood it, shining, to the flight
  of dragonflies and bees.
On the shore a forester was felling birches with a shot
  of his gun before his eyeless wife could kneel before
  him.
A pitch burner walked through fir woods conducting
  behind his thurible, which smelled of myrrh and
  juniper, compliant swarms migrating from forest
  nests and from mossy black holes.
Nearer, a child herding a path amidst ferns got lost
  between a beech and its shadow
and he alone saw how the first voice changed into a roe
and how the flight of a heron turned over the clouds,
  to show people their skyward gilded top.

1937

MIECZYSŁAW JASTRUN
(1903–1983)

JASTRUN has always stood apart from the quarrels of literary schools, though in his youth he was close to *Skamander*. I would call him a meditative or elegiac poet. His translations from Rilke prove his affinity with the lonely man of German letters. His vocation was to contemplate time and transience, but the history of Europe assigned his life another course. He survived, in Warsaw, several years of the Nazi occupation, endangered every minute because of his Jewish origin. He was then publishing his poems in resistance periodicals; since then his poetry has reflected the despair of a man who has witnessed the crime of genocide. Delicate, frail, tenderhearted, Jastrun is torn between his deepest urges, which are basically metaphysical, and his will to moral or political commitments. This is not the first time this dilemma has appeared in Polish poetry. When, after the war, he dedicated himself to writing books on Polish literature of the past (among them a voluminous 'vie romancée' of Mickiewicz, which has been translated into many languages) he was searching for an answer to his own problems. This is also the reason for his loving preoccupation with the precursor of modern Polish poetry, Cyprian Norwid, whose philosophy of historical time as meaningful in spite of apparently useless martyrdom is vindicated in many of Jastrun's poems. The connivance of many writers with the terror in the postwar years added to his torment, and his poem 'Man' should be understood in this context.

Remembrance

WHEN the crowd surrounded those dragged to death
You heard voices sneering at them,
You heard a cry, you looked at living eyes.
The sky was burning. The breeze was filled with
    smoke.

And you have come back to your native land
As one comes back to life. You look: a flower
Is being born of earth, fertile, much too fertile.
Like remorse, the distant trace of smoke turns blue,
The smell of burning is dispelled.
Shadows are pale.

The fragrance in the air is like a preparation
For new stems, for not-yet-spoken words.
The chestnuts are in bloom, and in the rusty wounds
Of earth, grass is at work, stitching up the web.
Buds are gluey, and in hazel thickets
The sound of water once again.

For whom is delight? Revelation of strength?
For whom is the nightingale in the tangle of young trees?
Its song erupts, breaks off, as if fountains
Of light were gushing up against the sky –

And far more hostile, more indifferent
than all that common and inhuman grave
is the beauty of the earth. And he that lost himself
. in the beauty of words as in some longed-for face –
his songs are pure, too pure. They will be overbalanced
by blood mixed with earth.

Man

I saw a man
Murdered by angels,
Tortured by questions,
Swollen by a strangled cry,
A live corpse,
A victim of morality.

And I could not help him,
Since he deserved no more than pity, which had been
    exiled,
And I had to give him the last blow
Together with the angels,
Trampling, tearing, butchering
His paltry heart,
His human – after all – heart.

A Woman Who Suddenly Entered the Room

In all your transparent pretence, in your painted hair
    and lips,
You are here, concealing within you another self, so
    real it hurts.
Trying to annihilate or at least neutralize your flesh,
Your nakedness, your entrails red with blood, your
    ovaries for conception,
Your vegetal-animal shape, the fruit of evolution and
    farfetched concepts of beauty.
But you can't hide your eyes, green insects with moving
    feelers,

And your white teeth which tear at animal meat.
At any moment we could return to the cave,
Children of the species and the war as we are,
Who have crawled out of the sea
Or fallen from the sky, in order to become again
After ages, seeds for other planets.

Beyond Time

I AM not concerned at all with the golden age of those
    pines
Or the white time of a carnation
Or the time of the dust on the highway
Or the time of passing clouds.
Whether I lived an age or an instant loses its importance.
It is enough to glance into the eyes of a sunflower,
To grind up thyme in your hand,
Any scent in the infinitive suffices,
Any of the usually unnoticed things of the earth,
Suddenly perceived in such a way
That their shape with eyelids not quite closed
Denies transience (of water, of clouds, of man).

WITOLD GOMBROWICZ
(1904–1969)

GOMBROWICZ would be amused to see his name in an anthology of poetry. Yet, though his admirers, both in Poland and abroad, have always considered him as a prose writer, some of his pages, especially in his voluminous *Diary* and in his plays, have the rhythms of poetry. He waged a war against modern poets, deriding their involuted style and their posturings as unrecognized geniuses. He never wrote poems himself.

Gombrowicz published two books before World War II. Shortly before its outbreak, in the summer of 1939, he left Poland on an excursion to Latin America, was stranded there, and lived for many years in Buenos Aires. In the 1960s he moved to France, where he died. In spite of a long time spent in a self-imposed exile, he preserved his masterful use of the Polish language and wrote only in Polish. The monologues I selected come from his play *The Marriage*, which he himself called the most important presentation of his philosophy. It is also one of the most complex and difficult works of that philosophic writer who, though often labeled by critics as 'existentialist' or 'structuralist', shunned any 'isms'. For a long time hardly published in Poland, he is recognized there as a major twentieth-century figure in Polish letters. His novels *Ferdydurke*, *Pornografia*, and *Cosmos* are available in English translation. Louis Iribarne has translated two of his plays: *The Marriage* and *Operetta*.

Two Monologues from The Marriage

HENRY: . . . Oh, the insanities I took part in!

> Although I was the sanest . . . most sensible
> Most reasonable of men
> Others drove me to commit
> The grimmest, deadliest,
> Most maniacal, and yes, unbridled acts . . .

This raises a simple question: If for several years some-
one acts the part of a madman, is he not a madman? So
what if I'm sane if my actions are sick—eh, Johnny?
But those who drove me to commit insanities were
also sane

> And sensible
> And reasonable . . . Friends, comrades, brothers—
>   so much
> Sanity
> And such sickness? So much common sense
> And such madness? So much humanity

And inhumanity? So what if, alone, each of us is sensible,
level-headed, when together we are a monstrous, raving
madman who

> Wrestles, rants, and blindly
> Rushes forward, breaking his own bounds
> Ripping himself out of himself . . . Our madness
> Is outside us, out there . . . Out there
> Where I myself end, there begins

My unbridledness . . . And though I live in peace
Inside myself, still I wander outside myself
And in dark, wild spaces and nocturnal places
Give myself to some unbounded chaos!

(Act II)

HENRY (alone):

A game
Suppose it's just a game
But . . . what sort of game? Can such games be
    dangerous?
I would like to know the real power of words.
What is my own power?
A dream? That's right, a dream . . . child's
    play . . .

(*To a piece of furniture*) You're staring at me, aren't you?
I'm caught in a grid of glances, a precinct of looks, and
whatever I look at, looks back at me

Although I'm alone
Alone
Surrounded by silence . . . I stick out my arm.
    This common
Normal
Everyday gesture
Swells with importance because it's not intended
For anyone
I wiggle my fingers in the silence, and my self
Swells itself to become itself

45

Seed of my seed. I, I, I! I alone!
And yet if I, I, I am alone, why
(Let's try this for effect) am I not?

Does it matter (I ask) if I am center stage if I can
never be

Myself?
I alone.
I alone.

Now that you're alone, all alone, you might at least quit
this incessant recitation

This fabrication of words
This production of gestures

But even when you're alone, you pretend you're alone,
and you go on

(For once, just this once, try to be sincere)

Pretending to yourself
To be yourself

I alone
I alone (once more, for emphasis) . . . but from
        over there
Wailing, weeping, and blood, alas, and terror
Oh, never has any man had
To solve such insoluble problems

Or groaned a more terrible burden
Of pain and dishonor . . .

What should be my attitude, I wonder? What pose
should I adopt? Why, why

Before this vile, inhuman
Wretched world I might wrinkle my brow
Lift my arms to heaven, I might
Roll my hand into a fist or pass my palm
Across my wise and thoughtful brow
I
Yes, that's right, I . . . might be moved
To such poses . . . in your presence
For your benefit! But not my own! I don't need
Any poses! I don't feel
Anyone's pain! I only recite
My humanity! I don't exist
I haven't any 'I', alas, I forge myself
Outside myself, alas, alas, oh, the hollow
Empty orchestra of my 'alas', you well up
And sink back into my emptiness!

Oh, you pontificators!
(Be vehement, sarcastic when you say that)
With your mouths so full of morality
And self-righteousness (Now grimace
Mockingly, sardonically, and make a sweeping
    gesture of the hand)
What are all your books and philosophies

Articles and lectures
Systems and arguments
Definitions and observations
Visions, passions, revelations before
Before this mass of two billion people
Teeming in perpetual
Dark and raw, unbridled heat . . .
In vain your fly buzzes about the nose
Of that green and black abyss (Now let your
    laughter resound
Your private, discreet
Quiet, ineffable
Humanly human laughter . . .) While you out
    there
Persist in your endless posing
We go on pinching ourselves in the customary
    way
Beneath the bushes of our destiny.

(And now, to bring
This monologue to a close)

I reject every order, every concept
I distrust every abstraction, every doctrine
I don't believe in God or in Reason!
Enough of these gods! Give me man!
Let him be like me, troubled, immature
Confused, opaque, dark, unshaped
So I can dance, play, wrestle with him!
Pretend to him! Court him!
Rape him, love him, and always

Shape myself from him and through him
Celebrate my marriage in the sacred human
   church!

(Act III)
Translated by Louis Iribarne

ADAM WAŻYK
(1905–1982)

WAŻYK's early poems showed more resemblance to modern French poetry than to the work of his Polish contemporaries, and his metrical ingenuity was shaped to a large extent by Guillaume Apollinaire, whom he translated with great skill. Opposed both to *Skamander* and the First Vanguard, he was highly regarded by the Second Vanguard of the nineteen thirties. The social poetry then advocated by some critics did not appeal to him, however, and he judged it artistically doubtful. The crucial role of World War II in Polish poetry finds confirmation in Ważyk's work. In those years (which he spent in the Soviet Union) he purified his poetry of the excretions of Vanguard fashions, made it more simple and virile, without falling into journalism in verse. His poems written at the end of the war (for instance, 'Sketch for a Memoir' from 1944, when Ważyk returned to Poland as an officer of the Polish Communist army) illustrate, in their subject and form, the 'overcoming' of prewar sensibility that makes Polish poetry what it is today. Later, in the period of doctrinaire blackout, Ważyk was foolish enough to build up theories negating the essence of his poetry, but he was wise enough rarely to apply them in practice. He produced a fine version of Pushkin's *Eugene Onegin*, which is superior to other Polish versions of that poem. His 1955 'Poem for Adults' is said to have inaugurated the 'thaw'. Since that time Ważyk's poetry has been a return to the preoccupations of his youth, on a higher level of consciousness and technique, and to the Warsaw scenery of his adolescence. His metrical innovations and his agile mind, which is able to control his own oversophistication, have contributed to his renown. Poets of the Second Vanguard, like myself, owe a debt to him.

ADAM WAŻYK

Sketch for a Memoir

I LOVED my native city, as you do, as everyone does,
we talked under chestnut trees, were pierced by the
    whistle of locomotives,
an addict of green maps was planning departures aloud,
we were two or ten and not one of us
knew that we were growing in a pause between one war
    and another.

I praised the movement of imagination and sailed in an
    open poem,
the bells were ringing, the family sat at the table,
a lamp hung from the ceiling like framed fire.
That was long ago, I grew up, I swam in rivers and seas,
I travelled but little in my years of vulgar adventures,
a Parisian boulevard sprinkled me with the blood of its
    lights,
knocked me out, crushed me with its rush or its sad-
    ness –
instead of me someone was dying, someone enjoying
    life.

Years of affliction,
lacunae in memory,
between one war and another
my brother, unemployed, went crazy and jumped out
    the window.
I did not visit him in the morgue,
I wept only when I knelt before his drawer,
looking at trifles as useless as he was:
a lighter out of order, little inventions,

magic tricks which he liked very much –
for him they took the place of assonance and rhyme.

Not only that disturbed me –
furniture too, sumptuous draperies,
pederasts writing poems about angels,
everything in society that announced new war,
beautiful mythomaniacs with platinum hair,
dressed in the style of the Viennese Secession,
novels not written, stillborn,
boredom and emptiness foretelling war.

Conversations at supper or over vodka in bars,
iridescent words in which the chaos drones.
For in those years people of not quite bad will
had their minds filled with noise, a camouflage for
    reaction,
ideas got entangled like gods in the era of syncretism,
I knew a painter who for three hours
was able to talk nonsense without stopping,
others composed crosswords,
waited for a cataclysm
as for a monstrous group photograph in a flash of
    magnesium,
red Nostradamus.

A liar was among us disguised as a journalist,
an informer was a Schöngeist or a bohemian poet,
a pimp and a German agent posed as snobs,
no one knew what were other people's sources of
    income,
ten just men were dying in Spain.

ADAM WAŻYK

In those years I used to ask myself in the words of my
    elder brother:
how many times must one wake you up before you
    recognize your epoch?
I talked to myself in the voice of my brother the suicide,
yet my pen instead of writing was leaving only dashes
    and marks
moving like a seismograph on paper, till it burst.

We were waked up, people of not quite bad will,
or buried under the rubble of a house.
And many were waked up
to have their eyes sealed with the bandages of death
and to be put against the wall in paper shirts.

Entrenched on the Vistula, in theWarsaw foreground,
looking through binoculars at the other bank,
tomorrow to be overrun by our cannons' projectiles,
I recollect
the years which were also your years,
people of not quite bad will,
buried in my heart as if in a common grave.

An Attempt

You were sitting at your desk and you heard a woman's
    voice in the bathroom
You were flying over the desert between day and night
Like Lazarus returning from beyond the grave

you were entering a streetcar after a long illness
You stood on many bridges over many rivers
All this is a truth but a non-continuous truth

An old watch
A bakelite casing from the cone of a grenade
souvenirs are for establishing your continuity in time
but nothing sticks together they are without power
inefficient fetishes

You are not hidden in objects
but between
like a forest spirit in the forest

You remember an empty moment
when you looked at a young grove
but you do not remember the hours of terror

A Search

THERE are people whom I meet every dozen years or so
there are others whom I remember without reason
I do not know whether they live but if they live
we pass each other like the blind

I see those who move merrily about
in rags of memories as in magnificent furs
fire unites with water dates went crazy
the verdigris is the oasis of the green

I would like to find somebody who knows well how it
    was
a little man familiar with the first grass
I saw him recently from afar he disappeared in the
    crowd
he was even smaller than before

A Pre-Columbian Sculpture

I N the Museum of Man
there is a face of a cruel god
hidden behind a face torn off a victim,
an invisible face
which can be recognized
by its doubled lips.
There I should have understood everything –
the ritual of a masquerade
and the sadness of a passer-by
the sadness of a passer-by stripped of his face.

January 1957

ANNA ŚWIRSZCZYŃSKA [SWIR]
(born 1909)

ANNA Świrszczyńska [Swir] was born in Warsaw, daughter of
a painter, and grew up in an artistic milieu. Her first volume,
short prose-poems published in 1936, secured for her the reputa-
tion of a refined craftswoman consciously drawing from medi-
eval Polish poetry and from the imagery of painting. The years
spent in Nazi-occupied Warsaw and her service as a military
nurse during the Warsaw Uprising of 1944 marked her pro-
foundly, but she found a form adequate to those experiences
only many years later. As she says herself, a writer has two basic
tasks: 'First, to create his/her own style. Second, to destroy
his/her own style. The second is more difficult'. She reached
her goal—a 'naked' style clinging to reality—late in life, in the
nineteen seventies, but those who knew her early poetry recog-
nized an internal logic in her development. In her mature phase
she is the author of violently feministic poems as well as of
brutal erotic poems of a rare concision. Her chronicle of the
Warsaw Uprising composed of tense descriptive poems, *Building
the Barricade*, appeared in 1972. (In 1979 a bilingual edition, with
a translation into English by Magnus J. Krynski and Robert A.
Maguire, was issued in Cracow.) She is fierce, lucid, ecstatic,
terrifying. Though recognized as an eminent poet, she occupies
a place somehow apart, perhaps because she often disconcerts
critics.

ANNA ŚWIRSZCZYŃSKA

I Knocked My Head Against the Wall

As a child
I put my finger in the fire
to become
a saint.

As a teenager
every day I would knock my head against the wall.

As a young girl
I went out through a window of a garret
to the roof
in order to jump.

As a woman
I had lice all over my body.
They cracked when I was ironing my sweater.

I waited sixty minutes
to be executed.
I was hungry
for six years.

Then I bore a child,
they were carving me
without putting me to sleep.

Then a thunderbolt killed me
three times
and I had to rise from the dead three times
without anyone's help.

Now I am resting
after three resurrections.

I Am Panting

WHY talk
if one can shout
why walk
if one can run
why live
if one can burn.

I am running and screaming from joy
I am running and screaming from despair
I am panting
my lungs work like crazy.

Violent feelings
are good, so I have heard, for your health.

Kill Me

DON'T kiss me, my love.
Don't hug me, my love.
If you love me
kill me, my love.

A Woman Talks to Her Thigh

IT is only thanks to your good looks
I can take part
in the rites of love.

Mystical ecstasies,
treasons delightful
as a crimson lipstick,
a perverse rococo
of psychological involutions,
sweetness of carnal longings
that take your breath,
pits of despair
sinking to the very bottom of the world:
all this I owe to you.

How tenderly I should every day
lash you with a whip of cold water,
if you alone allow me to possess
beauty and wisdom
irreplaceable.

The souls of my lovers
open to me in a moment of love
and I have them in my dominion.

I look as does a sculptor
at his work
at their faces snapped shut with eyelids,
martyred by ecstasy,
made dense
by happiness.
I read as does an angel
thoughts in their skulls,
I feel in my hand

a beating human heart,
I listen to the words
which are whispered by one human being to another
in the frankest moment of one's life.

I enter their souls,
I wander
by a road of delight or of horror
to lands as inconceivable
as the bottoms of the oceans.
Later on, heavy with treasures
I am coming slowly back
to myself.

Oh, many riches,
many precious truths
growing immense in a metaphysical echo,
many initiations
delicate and startling
I owe to you, my thigh.

The most exquisite refinement of my soul
would not give me any of those treasures
if not for the clear, smooth charm
of an amoral little animal.

ANNA ŚWIRSZCZYŃSKA

Song of Plenitude

PLENITUDE, oh what a plenitude.
Strength, oh what a strength.
I am full as if I were a pregnant star,
I am strong as if I could exist
all alone in space.

Out of suffering joy arose,
I have suffered, therefore I have the right
to exist so strongly.
I have gone through hell, therefore today I enter
the heaven of serenity,
a round heaven of a strong serenity,
of a serenity growing in power,
of a power growing in power,
as if into a voice of a pipe organ,
as if into an expanding inundation of light.
I enter into a lasting light.

That light is singing,
I am singing
I am one of a million voices,
one of a million rays,
I am shining. The situation
is indecently mystical,
I can't help it, I say how it is.

Light flows from my body,
from my head, from my doubled breast.

From the ten fingers of my hands,
from the ten toes of my feet
light flows.
I am spilled around,
I am spun out, I am spread about,
my skin disappears,
I fuse with things that are not me,
I dissolve in everything.
Once dissolved in anything
I don't exist,
that is I exist in an indescribably powerful manner.

This is death and immortality,
this is, maybe, Nirvana.
I apologize for that word but really this is it.

She Does Not Remember

SHE was an evil stepmother.
In her old age she is slowly dying
in an empty hovel.
She shudders
like a handful of burnt paper.
She does not remember that she was evil.
But she knows
that she feels cold.

ANNA ŚWIRSZCZYŃSKA

The Second Madrigal

A night of love
exquisite as a
concert from old Venice
played on exquisite instruments.
Healthy as a
buttock of a little angel.
Wise as an
ant-hill.
Garish as air
blown into a trumpet.
Abundant as a
reigning upon two thrones
cast in gold
of a Negro royal couple.

A night of love with you,
a big baroque battle
and two victories.

The Old Woman

HER beauty
is like Atlantis.
It is yet to be discovered.
Thousands of humorists
have written on her erotic desires.
The most gifted of them
entered the school reading lists.

64

Only her making love with the devil
had a seriousness
of fire around the stake
and was within the human imagination just as was
　　　that fire.

Mankind created for her
the most abusive
words of the world.

The Same Inside

WALKING to your place for a love feast
I saw at a street corner
an old beggar woman.

I took her hand
kissed her delicate cheek,
we talked, she was
the same inside as I am,
from the same kind,
I sensed this instantly
as a dog knows by its scent
another dog.

I gave her money,
I could not part from her.
After all, one needs
someone who is close.

And then I no longer knew
why I was walking to your place.

ANNA ŚWIRSZCZYŃSKA

From Building the Barricade

Building the Barricade

WE were afraid as we built the barricade
under fire.

The tavern-keeper, the jeweler's mistress, the barber,
all of us cowards.
The servant-girl fell to the ground
as she lugged a paving stone, we were terribly afraid
all of us cowards—
the janitor, the market-woman, the pensioner.

The pharmacist fell to the ground
as he dragged the door of a toilet,
we were even more afraid, the smuggler-woman,
the dressmaker, the streetcar driver,
all of us cowards.

A kid from reform school fell
as he dragged a sandbag,
you see we were really
afraid.

Though no one forced us,
we did build the barricade
under fire.

Translated by Magnus Jan Krynski
and Robert A. Maguire

FROM *Building the Barricade*

He Steals Furs

A shell tears apart the door
of the furrier's shop.

A man leaps in,
grabs an armful of furs,
lugs them to the gateway at a run.

At the gateway another shell
tears apart the man.

Translated by Magnus Jan Krynski
and Robert A. Maguire

Two Hunchbacks

'I can't afford to die, ma'm,
what would my sister do without me.
She's a hunchback, she's lying there by the window'.

'I can't afford to die, ma'm,
what would my sister do without me.
She's a hunchback, she's lying there by the door'.

Each of them died
of the wound of her sister
died the death of her hunchbacked sister.

Translated by Magnus Jan Krynski
and Robert A. Maguire

A Woman Said to Her Neighbor

A woman said to her neighbor:
'Since my husband was killed I can't sleep,
when there's shooting I dive under the blanket,

67

I tremble all night long under the blanket.
I'll go crazy if I have to be alone today,
I have some cigarettes my husband left, please
do drop in tonight'.

Translated by Magnus Jan Krynski
and Robert A. Maguire

It Smashes Barricades

ALONG a street swept clean of people
a tank rolls firing.
It executes
houses
smashes
barricades.

Out of the gateway leaps a kid
a bottle of gasoline in his fist.
Along the street swept clean of people
he runs
at a crouch
at the tank.

Translated by Magnus Jan Krynski
and Robert A. Maguire

Twenty of My Sons

IN my ward
lie twenty soldiers' bellies.
Ripped open, bloody,
fighting fiercely
for life.

FROM *Building the Barricade*

I know them all by heart,
by day I bring them bedpans, wash off the excrement.
By night I dream
that I bring them bedpans,
wash off the excrement.

When one of the bellies
dies in my dream
I wake with a start
and go up to the bed on tiptoe.

In my ward
fighting tooth and nail against nothingness are
twenty of my sons.

Translated by Magnus Jan Krynski
and Robert A. Maguire

I've Been Waiting These Thirty Years

THAT young beanpole was maybe six feet tall,
that light-hearted worker from Powiśle
who fought
in the hell on Zielna Street, in the telephone building.
When I changed the bandage on
his leg that was torn open
he winced, he laughed.

'When the war's over
we'll go dancing, miss.
It's on me'.

I've been waiting for him
these thirty years.

Translated by Magnus Jan Krynski
and Robert A. Maguire

ANNA ŚWIRSZCZYŃSKA

From the Author

THE Warsaw Uprising was one of the most tragic
events of World War II. The destruction it brought to a
city of more than a million people can only be compared
to the destruction visited on Hiroshima. Warsaw was
transformed into a wasteland filled with corpses, ruins
and smouldering ashes. That part of the population
which survived the inferno was driven out and de-
ported to various concentration camps. After the capit-
ulation, German soldiers systematically burned and
dynamited the remaining buildings. Himmler said:
'Warsaw must be levelled to the ground, in order to
set a deterring example for the whole of Europe'.

The priceless cultural heritage that had been accumu-
lated in Warsaw over the centuries by countless genera-
tions of Poles was completely destroyed. The splendid
palaces, the Castle of the Polish Kings, the historic
churches, the rich collections of art, the museums, the
libraries—all were turned into ashes and rubble. The
flower of the young intelligentsia, who had been raised
in a romantic love of freedom, perished. So did thou-
sands of heroic children, the world's youngest soldiers
at twelve and thirteen: with unexampled courage they
threw themselves at the tanks, gasoline bombs in hand,
and carried dispatches under a hail of bullets. The Ger-
man army that fought the insurrectionists was very
well-equipped; it had bombers, tanks, self-propelled
guns and flame-throwers. The insurrectionists had few
weapons, limited mainly to pistols and grenades. People
for whom even these weapons were in short supply
often took them from the enemy with their bare hands.
The insurrectionists suffered from hunger and cold;

they had no medicines nor bandages. Despite every-
thing, they fought heroically, in the belief that fervor
and self-sacrifice would make up for the overwhelming
strength of the enemy.

Life in Warsaw during the Uprising had the quality
of a nightmare. The city was deprived of water, elec-
tricity, gas and food supplies. The sewer system was
largely inoperative. Hospitals lacked medicines or pure
water. German bombers rampaged over the city day
and night, burying the living beneath the rubble. People
sought shelter from the air raids in basements, but found
no safety even there: the Germans dragged them out
and conducted mass executions—of men, women and
children. The Nazi tanks that rolled through the streets
spread death and destruction. The insurrectionists and
the population at large tried to defend themselves by
building barricades. Everyone joined in this under-
taking, regardless of age or sex. People did not sleep,
eat or wash for days on end. No one knew whether he
would be alive five minutes later. Corpses lay about in
the streets, and the stench of rotting bodies rose from
the ruins. Despite these horrible conditions, the city
put up a heroic struggle for sixty-three days. The in-
surrectionists and the population at large displayed an
extraordinary moral courage. But faced with the lack
of food, weapons and ammunition, Warsaw finally had
to surrender.

Translated by Magnus Jan Krynski
and Robert A. Maguire

CZESŁAW MIŁOSZ
(born 1911)

MILOSZ started to publish in the early nineteen thirties and was considered one of the leaders of the Second Vanguard. A movement turning away from both *Skamander* and the First Vanguard, the Second Vanguard was a reaction against the narrowness of quarrels centered around form. Because of the Cassandra-like prophecies in their poems, Milosz and his group were branded 'catastrophists'. The landscape of his native Lithuania has always been at the core of Milosz's imagery. Under the Nazi occupation, he edited a clandestinely printed anthology of anti-Nazi poems in Warsaw, and wrote his 'Voices of Poor Men', dedicated to the victims of oppression. The term 'classicism' applied to his poetry probably means that his experimentation is mitigated by an attachment to old Polish verse. His poetic work presents a great variety of forms ranging from mock odes and treatises in the spirit of the eighteenth century to notebooks of dreams. Some critics see in him a symbolist in reverse: in symbolism a poet proceeds from external reality towards the ineffable veiled by it, while Milosz circumvents with his symbols the essential being of things, which seems to be his main concern. He himself says his best poems are childishly naïve descriptions of things. Yet because of his civic passions he has always been the victim of a dichotomy. In 1948 he published a 'Treatise on Morals' in iambic verse deriding the rule by terror. He left Poland in the beginning of 1951 and lived for ten years as a freelance in Paris where he wrote several books in prose, among them *The Captive Mind*. Since 1961 he has been Professor of Slavic Languages and Literatures at the University of California, Berkeley. In 1978 he was awarded the Neustadt International Prize for Literature; in 1980 he received the Nobel Prize.

Dedication

YOU whom I could not save
Listen to me.
Try to understand this simple speech as I would be
  ashamed of another.
I swear, there is in me no wizardry of words.
I speak to you with silence like a cloud or a tree.

What strengthened me, for you was lethal.
You mixed up farewell to an epoch with the beginning
  of a new one,
Inspiration of hatred with lyrical beauty,
Blind force with accomplished shape.

Here is the valley of shallow Polish rivers. And an
  immense bridge
Going into white fog. Here is a broken city,
And the wind throws screams of gulls on your grave
When I am talking with you.

What is poetry which does not save
Nations or people?
A connivance with official lies,
A song of drunkards whose throats will be cut in a
  moment,
Readings for sophomore girls.
That I wanted good poetry without knowing it,
That I discovered, late, its salutary aim,
In this and only this I find salvation.

They used to pour on graves millet or poppy seeds
To feed the dead who would come disguised as birds.
I put this book here for you, who once lived
So that you should visit us no more.

1945

A Poor Christian Looks at the Ghetto

BEES build around red liver,
Ants build around black bone.
It has begun: the tearing, the trampling on silks,
It has begun: the breaking of glass, wood, copper, nickel,
    silver, foam
Of gypsum, iron sheets, violin strings, trumpets, leaves,
    balls, crystals.
Poof! Phosphorescent fire from yellow walls
Engulfs animal and human hair.

Bees build around the honeycomb of lungs,
Ants build around white bone.
Torn is paper, rubber, linen, leather, flax,
Fibre, fabrics, cellulose, snakeskin, wire.
The roof and the wall collapse in flame and heat seizes
    the foundations.
Now there is only the earth, sandy, trodden down,
With one leafless tree.

Slowly, boring a tunnel, a guardian mole makes his way,
With a small red lamp fastened to his forehead.
He touches burned bodies, counts them, pushes on,

75

He distinguishes human ashes by their luminous vapour,
The ashes of each man by a different part of the spec-
    trum.
Bees build around a red trace.
Ants build around the place left by my body.

I am afraid, so afraid of the guardian mole.
He has swollen eyelids, like a Patriarch
Who has sat much in the light of candles
Reading the great book of the species.
What will I tell him, I, a Jew of the New Testament,
Waiting two thousand years for the second coming of
    Jesus?
My broken body will deliver me to his sight
And he will count me among the helpers of death:
The uncircumcised.

1943

A Song on the End of the World

On the day the world ends
A bee circles a clover,
A fisherman mends a glimmering net.
Happy porpoises jump in the sea,
By the rainspout young sparrows are playing
And the snake is gold-skinned as it should always be.

On the day the world ends
Women walk through the fields under their umbrellas,
A drunkard grows sleepy at the edge of a lawn,

FROM 'THROUGHOUT OUR LANDS'

Vegetable peddlers shout in the street
And a yellow-sailed boat comes nearer the island,
The voice of a violin lasts in the air
And leads into a starry night.

And those who expected lightning and thunder
Are disappointed.
And those who expected signs and archangels' trumps
Do not believe it is happening now.
As long as the sun and the moon are above,
As long as the bumblebee visits a rose,
As long as rosy infants are born
No one believes it is happening now.

Only a white-haired old man, who would be a prophet
Yet is not a prophet, for he's much too busy,
Repeats while he binds his tomatoes:
There will be no other end of the world,
There will be no other end of the world.

1944

From 'Throughout Our Lands'

III

If I had to tell what the world is for me
I would take a hamster or a hedgehog or a mole
and place him in a theatre seat one evening
and, bringing my ear close to his humid snout,
would listen to what he says about the spotlights,
sounds of the music, and movements of the dance.

VII

With their chins high, girls come back from the tennis
    courts.
The spray rainbows over the sloping lawns.
With short jerks a robin runs up, stands motionless.
The eucalyptus tree trunks glow in the light.
The oaks perfect the shadow of May leaves.
Only this. Only this is worthy of praise: the day.

But beneath it elemental powers are turning somer-
    saults;
and devils, mocking the naïve who believe in them,
play catch with hunks of bloody meat,
whistle songs about matter without beginning or end,
and about the moment of our agony
when everything we have cherished will appear
an artifice of cunning self-love.

VIII

And what if Pascal had not been saved
and if those narrow hands in which we laid a cross
are just he, entire, like a lifeless swallow
in the dust, under the buzz of the poisonous-blue flies?

And if they all, kneeling with poised palms,
millions, billions of them, ended together with their
    illusion?
I shall never agree. I will give them the crown.
The human mind is splendid; lips, powerful,
and the summons, so great, it must open Paradise.

IX

They are so persistent, that give them a few stones
and edible roots, and they will build the world.

XI

Paulina, her room behind the servants' quarters, with one
    window on the orchard
where I gather the best apples near the pigsty
squishing with my big toe the warm muck of the dung-
    hill,
and the other window on the well (I love to drop the
    bucket down
and scare its inhabitants, the green frogs).
Paulina, a geranium, the chill of a dirt floor,
a hard bed with three pillows,
an iron crucifix and images of the saints
decorated with palms and paper roses.
Paulina died long ago, but is.
And, I am somehow convinced, not just in my con-
    sciousness.

Above her rough Lithuanian peasant face
hovers a spindle of hummingbirds, and her flat calloused
    feet
are sprinkled by sapphire water in which dolphins
with their backs arching
frolic.

XIV

Cabeza, if anyone knew all about civilization, it was you.
A bookkeeper from Castile, what a fix you were in
to have to wander about, where no notion,

no cipher, no stroke of a pen dipped in sepia,
only a boat thrown up on the sand by surf,
crawling naked on all fours, under the eye of immobile
        Indians,
and suddenly their wail in the void of sky and sea,
their lament: that even the gods are unhappy.
For seven years you were their predicted god,
bearded, white-skinned, beaten if you couldn't work a
        miracle.
Seven years' march from the Mexican Gulf to Cali-
        fornia,
the hu-hu-hu of tribes, hot bramble of the continent.
But afterwards? Who am I, the lace of cuffs
not mine, the table carved with lions not mine, Doña
        Clara's
fan, the slipper from under her gown – hell, no.
On all fours! On all fours!
Smear our thighs with war paint.
Lick the ground. Wha wha, hu hu.

Translated by Peter Dale Scott
and the author

Advice

YES, it is true that the landscape changed a little.
Where there were forests, now there are pears of
        factories, gas tanks.
Approaching the mouth of the river we hold our noses.

ADVICE

Its current carries oil and chlorine and methyl com-
pounds,
Not to mention the by-products of the Books of Ab-
straction:
Excrement, urine, and dead sperm.
A huge stain of artificial colour poisons fish in the sea.
Where the shore of the bay was overgrown with rushes
Now it is rusted with smashed machines, ashes and
bricks.
We used to read in old poets about the scent of earth
And grasshoppers. Now we bypass the fields:
Ride as fast as you can through the chemical zone of the
farmers.
The insect and the bird are extinguished. Far away a
bored man
Drags dust with his tractor, an umbrella against the sun.
What do we regret? – I ask. A tiger? A shark?
We created a second Nature in the image of the first
So as not to believe that we live in Paradise.
It is possible that when Adam woke in the garden
The beasts licked the air and yawned, friendly,
While their fangs and their tails, lashing their backs,
Were figurative and the red-backed shrike,
Later, much later, named Lanius Collurio,
Did not impale caterpillars on spikes of the blackthorn.
However, other than that moment, what we know of
Nature
Does not speak in its favour. Ours is no worse.
So I beg you, no more of those lamentations.

From 'Bobo's Metamorphosis'

VII

BOBO, a nasty boy, was changed into a fly.
In accordance with the rite of the flies he washed him-
  self by a rock of sugar
And ran vertically in caves of cheese.
He flew through a window into the bright garden.
There, indomitable ferryboats of leaves
Carried a drop taut with the excess of its rainbow,
Mossy parks grew by ponds of light in the mountains of
  bark,
An acrid dust fell from flexible columns inside cinnabar
  flowers.
And though it did not last longer than from tea time till
  supper,
Later on, when he wore pressed trousers and a trimmed
  moustache,
He always thought, holding a glass of liquor, that he was
  cheating them
For a fly should not discuss the nation and productivity.
A woman facing him was a volcanic peak
Where there were ravines, craters and in hollows of lava
The movement of earth was tilting crooked trunks of
  pines.

V

I liked him as he did not look for an ideal object.
When he heard: 'only the object which does not exist
Is perfect and pure', he blushed and turned away.

In every pocket he carried pencils, pads of paper
Together with crumbs of bread, the accidents of life.

Year after year he circled a thick tree
Shading his eyes with his hand and muttering admiringly.

How much he envied those who draw a tree with one
line!
But metaphor seemed to him something indecent.

He would leave symbols to the proud busy with their
cause.
By looking he wanted to draw the name from the very
thing.
When he was old, he tugged at his tobacco-stained beard:
'I prefer to lose thus than to win as they do.'

Like Peter Breughel the father he fell suddenly
While attempting to look back between his spread-apart
legs.

And still there stood the tree unattainable.
O veritable, o true to the very core. It was.

VIII

Between her and me there was a table, on the table a
glass.
The chapped skin of her elbows touched the shining
surface
In which the contour of shade under her armpit was
reflected.
A drop of sweat thickened over her wavy lip.
And the space between her and me fractionized itself
infinitely

Buzzing with feathered Eleatic arrows.
Not a year, not a hundred years of journey would exhaust it.
Had I overturned the table what would we have accomplished?
That act, a non-act, always no more than potential
Like the attempt to penetrate water, wood, minerals,
But she, too, looked at me as if I were a ring of Saturn
And knew I was aware that no one attains.
Thus were posited humanness, tenderness.

TADEUSZ RÓŻEWICZ
(born 1921)

RÓŻEWICZ's poetry stems from traumatic war experiences. He served in the guerrilla Home Army and his first poems published immediately after the war are short, nearly stenographic notes of horror, disgust, and derision at human values. Long before anybody in Poland had heard of Samuel Beckett, Różewicz's imagination created equally desperate landscapes. Since he hated art as an offence to human suffering, he invented his own type of anti-poem, stripped of 'devices' such as metre, rhyme, and even, most often, of metaphors, and limited to the simplest words. His scorn for 'art' is quite programmatic, with all the contradictions such an attitude involves. He is a nihilistic humanitarian, constantly searching for a way out of his negation which is mitigated only by pity; his tenderness bursts out only when he writes on little things of everyday life. He was unsuccessful in his attempts to find solace in an ideology. His poems written between 1949 and 1956, when he tried to sound positive and optimistic, fell often into what he had avoided before and has avoided since, sentimentality. It seems that his tragedy is to deny the values which are affirmed by his revolt. It is not by chance that I have mentioned Beckett. Różewicz is the author of a few plays which exemplify the Polish 'theatre of the absurd'. The target of his attacks is the precarious normality undermined by chaos and violence; and the title of one of his plays is, significantly enough, 'The Witnesses, or Our Little Stabilization'. The impact of his 'naked' poetry upon the younger writers has been universally recognized. He lives in Gliwice, an industrial town of Silesia.

TADEUSZ RÓŻEWICZ

In the Middle of Life

AFTER the end of the world
after my death
I found myself in the middle of life
I created myself
constructed life
people animals landscapes

this is a table I was saying
this is a table
on the table are lying bread a knife
the knife serves to cut the bread
people nourish themselves with bread

one should love man
I was learning by night and day
what one should love
I answered man

this is a window I was saying
this is a window
beyond the window is a garden
in the garden I see an apple tree
the apple tree blossoms
the blossoms fall off
the fruits take form
they ripen my father is picking up an apple
that man who is picking up an apple
is my father

I was sitting on the threshold of the house

that old woman who
is pulling a goat on a rope
is more necessary
and more precious
than the seven wonders of the world
whoever thinks and feels
that she is not necessary
he is guilty of genocide

this is a man
this is a tree this is bread

people nourish themselves in order to live
I was repeating to myself
human life is important
human life has great importance
the value of life
surpasses the value of all the objects
which man has made
man is a great treasure
I was repeating stubbornly

this is water I was saying
I was stroking the waves with my hand
and conversing with the river
water I said
good water
this is I

the man talked to the water
talked to the moon
to the flowers to the rain
he talked to the earth
to the birds
to the sky

the sky was silent
the earth was silent
if he heard a voice
which flowed
from the earth from the water from the sky
it was the voice of another man

The Apple

GIVE me an apple
said the husband
and stretched out his hand

from a clay bowl
a snake was sipping milk
a domestic gentle snake
black with orange
lightning

in the cradle a little man
was sucking the big toe of his foot
larger
than the flower called 'lady's slipper'.

A spider tied together
the hands of the clock
which ticked out eternity
to the happy

and when the weak thread snapped
the wife handed the red apple
to her husband
and quiet
sat down on the threshhold
of the family nest

Playing Horses

THE canary yellow
as a lemon
in a wire basket

the grandmother in a bonnet
all caught
in a net of wrinkles

the father with his brow hidden
in a cloud of smoke

the boys neigh
loose their manes in the wind
beat their hoofs
against the impatient ground

the mother has captured
a magnificent steed
in white suspenders
and is kissing his sour mouth
full of sorrel

The Wall

SHE turned her face to the wall

yet she loves me
why did she turn away from me

so with such a motion of one's head
one can turn away from the world
where sparrows are chirping
and young people are walking
in their garish neckties

She is now alone
in the presence of the dead wall
and she will remain so

she will remain against the wall
which will grow bigger and bigger
coiled up and small
with a clenched fist

and I am sitting
with stony feet
I do not carry her away from that place
I do not lift her
Who is lighter than a sigh

A Voice

THEY mutilate they torment each other
with silences with words
as if they had another
life to live

they do so
as if they had forgotten
that their bodies
are inclined to death
that the insides of men
easily break down

ruthless with each other
they are weaker
than plants and animals
they can be killed by a word
by a smile by a look

Albumen

THEY pat the sick man on the head
like a good dog

they talk to him
as to a child
touch his body
exchange
knowing looks

the sick man hears
everything understands
endures

he bites nobody's hand
he is so well behaved
that he'll even believe in the angel
he swallows a raw egg
on a moonlight night
the colour of albumen

beyond the open window
translucent jasmines bloom

a young nurse
with two breasts
two hands four legs
is turning her back

the sick man gnashing his teeth
asks
close the window please

Transformations

My little son enters
the room and says
'you are a vulture
I am a mouse'

I put away my book
wings and claws
grow out of me

their ominous shadows
race on the walls
I am a vulture
he is a mouse

'you are a wolf
I am a goat'
I walked around the table
and am a wolf
windowpanes gleam
like fangs
in the dark

while he runs to his mother
safe
his head hidden in the warmth of her dress

Leave Us Alone

FORGET about us
about our generation
live like human beings
forget about us

we envied
plants and stones
we envied dogs

I would like to be a rat
I used to say to her

I would like not to be
I would like to fall asleep
and wake up after the war
she would say with her eyes shut

forget about us
don't ask about our youth
leave us alone

The Deposition of the Burden

HE came to us
and said

you are not responsible
either for the world or for the end of the world
the burden is taken from your shoulders
you are like birds and children
play

and they play

they forget
that modern poetry
is a struggle for breath

To the Heart

I saw
a cook a specialist
he would put his hand
into the mouth
and through the trachea
push it to the inside
of a sheep
and there in the quick
would grasp the heart
tighten his grip
on the heart
rip out the heart
in one jerk
yes
that was a specialist

TADEUSZ RÓŻEWICZ

A Sketch for a Modern Love Poem

AND yet whiteness
can be best described by greyness
a bird by a stone
sunflowers
in december

love poems of old
used to be descriptions of flesh
they described this and that
for instance eyelashes

and yet redness
should be described
by greyness the sun by rain
the poppies in november
the lips at night

the most palpable
description of bread
is that of hunger
there is in it
a humid porous core
a warm inside
sunflowers at night
the breasts the belly the thighs of Cybele

a transparent
source-like description
of water
is that of thirst

A SKETCH FOR A MODERN LOVE POEM

of ash
of desert
it provokes a mirage
clouds and trees enter
a mirror of water
lack hunger
absence
of flesh
is a description of love
in a modern love poem

TYMOTEUSZ KARPOWICZ
(born 1921)

FEW people heard of Karpowicz before 1956–57 except as one of the young writers who settled in Silesia. His poetry matured slowly and in secret. Perhaps his is the case of a life on two levels, or of walking with a mask. A journalist, the editor of a weekly magazine in Wrocław, he preserved an 'inner freedom' from the pressures of actuality. He has faithful but not numerous admirers, as his poetry is sometimes very difficult because of its conciseness. It can be compared to miniature ink drawings. This is not to say that his range is limited. For instance, his short poem 'A Lesson of Silence' is the transposed image of a whole era, and an excellent German translator of Polish poetry, Karl Dedecius, gave his anthology a title borrowed from that poem. I would be inclined, however, to look at Karpowicz primarily as a poet of love: he is in love with Earth. An intimate relationship with trees, flowers and animals is probably his strength, and a guarantee of independence. These last years he has been professor of Polish literature at the University of Illinois.

The Pencil's Dream

WHEN the pencil undresses for sleep
he firmly decides
to sleep stiffly
and blackly

he is helped in it
by the inborn inflexibility
of all the piths of the world
the spinal pith of the pencil
will break but cannot be bent

he will never dream of
waves or hair
only of a soldier standing at attention
or coffins

what finds its place in him
is straight
what is beyond is crooked
good night

A Lesson of Silence

WHENEVER a butterfly
happened to fold
too violently its wings –
there was a call: silence, please!

LOVE

As soon as one feather
of a startled bird
jostled against a ray –
there was a call: silence, please!

In that way were taught
how to walk without noise
the elephant on his drum,
man on his earth.

The trees were rising
mute above the fields
as rises the hair
of the horror-stricken.

Love

I believed:
a tree when kissed
would not lose its leaves –
leaves fall
from kissed
trees.

A river hugged
by a hand in love
would not flow away –
it flows away
into fog.

There are in my landscape
errors of colours and scents
yet always
always I love
what incessantly
changes.

As a golden ball
she runs before me:
approached again and again,
my beloved,
Earth.

Turns

patiently
the earth turns
and the brass dregs of the movement
encrust by layers the door knob
more and more resistant is my door
beyond which animals glitter
birds bloom
trees swarm

having badly chosen
my kingdom on a cracked cloud
I will float today
over one more turn of the earth

later on – remember:
give to drink to my golden deer
and feed the birds
which I left
beyond the heavy door

MIRON BIAŁOSZEWSKI

(born 1922)

ALTHOUGH Białoszewski became the subject of a heated literary controversy in 1956, he was well known prior to that time in Warsaw literary circles for his vanguard theatre, which he directed in a private apartment; the plays were written and performed by himself and a few friends. He lived through years of dismal misery, like many other writers and painters who were rejected because of their hopeless oddity. His poetry pushes enmity toward eloquence to an extreme, and explores the life of the most undignified objects, which are associated with the greyness and monotony of everyday existence. He is a poet of dirty staircases, rusty pipes, old stoves, kitchen utensils, mouldy walls. His wild metaphors and his intent of revindicating the incongruous substance surrounding man shocked many readers, but in his recent poems he has gone further and experimented with the language, focusing his attention on morphological and semantic incongruities. He breaks up words into their components, combines components in a new way, invents fantastic declensions. In the nineteen twenties some poets proceeded in this direction, but for different reasons. They were hunting for sonorities, which are not Białoszewski's concern, for he is fascinated by ugly sibilants and ridiculously jarring sounds. He questions the communicative function of language, and substitutes for words mumblings and mutterings. Or perhaps, as somebody said, he wants to return to the awkwardness of medieval Polish. His work illustrates the profound changes in sensibility which relegate the era of *Skamander* to a remote past. I have limited myself to his earlier phase, as have Białoszewski's translators into French and German.

And Even, Even If They Take Away the Stove

My Inexhaustible Ode to Joy
I have a stove
similar to a triumphal arch!

They take away my stove
similar to a triumphal arch! !

Give me back my stove
similar to a triumphal arch! ! !

They took it away.
What remains is
a grey
      naked
           hole.

And this is enough for me;
grey naked hole
grey naked hole.
greynakedhole.

A Ballad of Going Down to the Store

FIRST I went down to the street
by means of the stairs,
just imagine it,
by means of the stairs.

Then people known to people unknown
passed me by and I passed them by.
Regret
that you did not see
how people walk,
regret!

I entered a complete store:
lamps of glass were glowing.
I saw somebody – he sat down –
and what did I hear? what did I hear?
rustling of bags and human talk.

And indeed,
indeed
I returned.

Garwolin – a Town for Ever

garlic like a pearl . . . why? garlic is but garlic

tiny umptytown
its winter is peeling

over the town
the sky of garlic
thence for the town
days are like garlic braids

don't you feel by chance
in those peels
the pressure of Roman legions?
and on the garlic flesh
a Spain skidding?
and in the bitterness of juice
a sophist?

Self-Portrait as Felt

THEY look at me
so probably I have a face.
Of all the faces known
I remember least my own.

Often my hands
live in absolute separation.
Should I then count them as mine?
Where are my limits?
I am overgrown by
movement or half-life.

Yet always is crawling in me
full or not full
existence.

I bear by myself
a place of my own.
When I lose it
it will mean I am not.

I am not,
so I do not doubt.

My Jacobean Fatigues

My Jacobs of Tiredness

HIGHER
clarion calls of form,
habitations of touch,
all serenities of senses.

Lowest of all, I.
From my breast they **grow**
stairs of reality.

And I feel nothing.
Nothing of juiciness.
Nothing of colour.
Not only am I not
one of the Testament heroes
but worse than a flounder
glued to the bottom to die
with balloons of breath
bubbling up in bundles,
worse than a potato mother
who put forth
enormous antlers of tubes
and herself is shrinking
up to disappearance.

Strike me
construction of my world!

WISŁAWA SZYMBORSKA
(born 1923)

IN the previous edition of this book I expressed certain misgivings as to Szymborska's 'playing with ideas borrowed from anthropology and philosophy', which might easily, I contended, make poetry dependent on intellectual fashions and encourage preciosity. Perhaps this is true of the weaker of her poems, but her best do not deserve that reproach, and her subsequent evolution as a poet has justly placed her quite high among her contemporaries. I like much of her bitter, skeptical, and witty verse and her honesty in voicing her rather desperate vision. In the previous edition she was represented by one poem only. I hope the new translations I am adding are not a love's labor lost.

I Am Too Near

I AM too near to be dreamt of by him.
I do not fly over him, do not escape from him
under the roots of a tree. I am too near.
Not in my voice sings the fish in the net,
not from my finger rolls the ring.
I am too near. A big house is on fire
without me, calling for help. Too near
for a bell dangling from my hair to chime.
Too near to enter as a guest
before whom walls glide apart by themselves.
Never again will I die so lightly,
so much beyond my flesh, so inadvertently
as once in his dream. Too near.
I taste the sound, I see the glittering husk of this word
as I lie immobile in his embrace. He sleeps,
more accessible now to her, seen but once,
a cashier of a wandering circus with one lion,
than to me, who am at his side.
For her now in him a valley grows,
rusty-leaved, closed by a snowy mountain
in the dark blue air. I am too near
to fall to him from the sky. My scream
could wake him up. Poor thing
I am, limited to my shape,
I who was a birch, who was a lizard,
who would come out of my cocoons
shimmering the colours of my skins. Who possessed
the grace of disappearing from astonished eyes,
which is a wealth of wealths. I am near,
too near for him to dream of me.

I slide my arm from under the sleeper's head
and it is numb, full of swarming pins,
on the tip of each, waiting to be counted,
the fallen angels sit.

A Great Number

FOUR billion people on this earth,
while my imagination remains as it was.
It clumsily copes with great numbers.
Still it is sensitive to the particular.
It flutters in the dark like a flashlight,
and reveals the first random faces
while all the rest stay unheeded,
unthought of, unlamented.
Yet even Dante could not retain all that.
And what of us?
Even all the Muses could not help.

Non omnis moriar—a premature worry.
Yet do I live entire and does it suffice?
It never sufficed, and especially now.
I choose by discarding, for there is no other means
but what I discard is more numerous,
more dense, more insistent than it ever was.
A little poem, a sigh, cost indescribable losses.
A thunderous call is answered by my whisper.
I cannot express how much I pass over in silence.
A mouse at the foot of a mountain in labor.
Life lasts a few marks of a claw on the sand.
My dreams—even they are not, as they ought to be,
    populous.

There is more of loneliness in them than of crowds
    and noise.
Sometimes a person who died long ago drops in for
    a moment.
A door handle moves touched by a single hand.
An empty house is overgrown with annexes of an
    echo.
I run from the threshhold down into the valley
that is silent, as if nobody's, anachronic.

How that open space is in me still—
I don't know.

The Joy of Writing

WHERE is a written deer running through a written
    forest?
Whether to drink from written water
which will reflect its mouth like a carbon?
Why is it raising its head, does it hear something?
Propped on four legs borrowed from the truth
it pricks up its ears from under my fingers.
Silence—that word, too, is rustling on paper
and parts the branches caused by the word 'forest'.

Over a white page letters are ready to jump
and they may take a bad turn.
Sentences capable of bringing to bay,
and against which there is no help.

UTOPIA

In a drop of ink there are quite a few
hunters squinting one eye,
ready to rush down a vertical pen,
to encircle the deer, to take aim.

They forget that this is not life here.
Other laws rule here, in black and white.
An instant will last as long as I desire.
It will allow a division into small eternities
each full of buckshot stopped in its flight.
If I command, nothing here will happen ever.
Not even a leaf will fall without my accord,
or a blade of grass bend under a dot of a hoof.

And so there is such a world
on which I impose an autonomous Fate?
A time which I bind with fetters of signs?
A life that at my command is perpetual?

The joy of writing.
A chance to make things stay.
A revenge of a mortal hand.

Utopia

An island where all is elucidated.

There, it is possible to stand on the ground of proofs.

No other roads there than the roads of arrival.

The bushes are heavily loaded with answers.

A tree is there of the Correct Guess
with branches disentangled for ever.

A dazzlingly simple tree of Comprehension
by a source which bears the name That's-how-it-is.

The further you advance, the larger it opens,
the Valley of Obviousness.

If any doubt appears, the wind dispells it.

The echo takes along a voice without being called
and willingly elucidates the secrets of the world.

To the right, a cave in which Meaning resides.

To the left a lake of Profound Conviction.

The Truth tears itself from the bottom and lithely
    flows to the surface.

The valley is dominated by Unshaken Certainty.
From its peak there is a view down on the Heart of
    the Matter.

In spite of its charms, the island is uninhabited,
and tiny traces of feet, visible near the shore,
without exception are turned toward the sea.

As if only departures were practiced there
in order to plunge irrevocably in the deep.

In life beyond understanding.

Autotomy

In danger the holothurian splits itself in two:
it offers one self to be devoured by the world
and in its second self escapes.

Violently it divides itself into a doom and a salvation,
into a penalty and a recompense, into what was and
    what will be.

In the middle of the holothurian's body a chasm opens
and its edges immediately become alien to each other.

On the one edge, death, on the other, life.
Here despair, there, hope.

If there is a balance, the scales do not move.
If there is justice, here it is.

To die as much as necessary, without overstepping
    the bounds.
To grow again from a salvaged remnant.

We, too, know how to split ourselves
but only into the flesh and a broken whisper.
Into the flesh and poetry.

On one side the throat, on the other, laughter,
slight, quickly calming down.

Here a heavy heart, there *non omnis moriar,*
three little words only, like three little plumes ascending.

The chasm doesn't split us.
A chasm surrounds us.

To the memory of Halina Poświatowska

Letters of the Dead

WE read letters of the dead and are like helpless gods,
yet gods after all, for we know what happened after.
We know what money has never been returned.
How quickly widows married and whom they
    married.
The poor dead, the infatuated dead,
deceived, erring, clumsily circumspect.
We see grimaces and signs made behind their backs.
Our ears catch the rustling of last wills torn to pieces.
They sit before us, comic, as if on open sandwiches
or rush forward chasing their hats snatched by the
    wind.
Their bad taste, Napoleon, steam and electricity,
their lethal cures for curable illnesses,
their foolish apocalypse according to Saint John
and a false paradise according to Jean-Jacques . . .
We observe in silence their pawns on a chessboard,
except that their pawns were moved three squares
    forward.
Everything they had foreseen happened in a
    completely different way,

or slightly different, which amounts to completely
    different.
The most zealous among them look with hope into
    our eyes
for by their calculations they should see in them
    perfection.

Every Case

IT could have happened.
It must have happened.
It happened earlier. Later.
Closer by. Further away.
It happened not to you.

You survived because you were the first.
You survived because you were the last.
Because you were alone. Because you were with
    others.
Because to the left. Because to the right.
Because it rained. Because there was shade.
Because the day was sunny.

Fortunately a forest was there.
Fortunately no trees were there.
Fortunately a rail, a hook, a bar, a brake,
an embrasure, a curve, a millimeter, a second.
Fortunately a razor was floating on water.

As a consequence, because, and yet, in spite.
What it would have been if a hand, a leg,
within an ace of, by a hair's breadth
saved from a combination of circumstances.

117

So you are here? Straight from an abrogated moment?
The net had just one mesh and you went through that
    mesh?
I am all surprise and all silence.
Listen,
how quickly your heart beats to me.

Laughter

A little girl that I was—
I, of course, know her.
I have a few photographs
from her short life.
I feel an amused pity
for a couple of her poems.
I remember a few events.

But
so that he who is here
will laugh and embrace me
I recollect just one little story:
a childish love
of that small ugly one.

I tell
how she was in love with a student
which means she wanted him to glance at her.

I tell
how she ran to meet him

with a bandage on her unhurt head
so that he at least, oh, would ask her
what had happened.

An amusing little one.
How could she know
that even despair brings profit
if by a happy chance
one manages to live longer.

I would send her away to buy a cookie for herself.
I would send her to the movies.
Go, I have no time.

Why, you can see
that the light is off,
you surely understand
that the door is locked.
Don't yank the door handle—
he who laughed now,
he who embraced me
is not your student.

You had better return
to where you came from.
I owe you nothing,
an ordinary woman
who knows only
in what moment
to betray somebody's secret.

Don't look at us
with those eyes of yours,
too widely open
like the eyes of the dead.

ZBIGNIEW HERBERT

(born 1924)

THE unusually large number of Herbert's poems in this anthology is due to the fact that they translate exceptionally well, because of their intellectual structure. There is also, of course, the deep affinity I feel with his writings. He was over thirty when his first book of poems appeared. Before 1956 the price for being published was to renounce one's own taste and he did not want to pay it. His personal qualities (good health, toughness, an orderly mind) helped him to survive the war when he was a member of the underground movement, and later, the period of required political orthodoxy. The form of his poetry shows the continuity of a line going from the pre-war Second Vanguard through Różewicz to younger poets, but his tone is unmistakable. If the key to contemporary Polish poetry is the collective experience of the last decades, Herbert is perhaps the most skilful in expressing it and can be called a poet of historical irony. He achieves a sort of precarious equilibrium by endowing the patterns of civilization with meanings, in spite of all its horrors. History for him is not just a senseless repetition of crimes and illusions, and if he looks for analogies between the past and the present, it is to acquire a distance from his own times. His theory of art is based upon the rejection of 'purity': to the imperturbable Apollo he opposes the howling, suffering Marsyas, though his own reticent poetry is the opposite of a howl. I should add that his solid humanist formation – he has a diploma in law, has studied philosophy and history of art – explains many themes in his poems. Written after two years spent in France and Italy, his essays (on the Albigenses, on the Templars, on the proportions of the Greek temples in Paestum, on the accounts of medieval masonic guilds) are linked organically to his poetry, as are his short plays. He lives in Warsaw but visits Western Europe from time to time.

ZBIGNIEW HERBERT

At the Gate of the Valley

AFTER the rain of stars
on the meadow of ashes
they all have gathered under the guard of angels

from a hill that survived
the eye embraces
the whole lowing two-legged herd

in truth they are not many
counting even those who will come
from chronicles fables and the lives of the saints

but enough of these remarks
let us lift our eyes
to the throat of the valley
from which comes a shout

after a loud whisper of explosion
after a loud whisper of silence
this voice resounds like a spring of living water
it is we are told
a cry of mothers from whom children are taken
since as it turns out
we shall be saved each one alone

the guardian angels are unmoved
and let us grant they have a hard job

she begs
– hide me in your eye
in the palm of your hand in your arms
we have always been together
you can't abandon me
now when I am dead and need tenderness

a higher ranking angel
with a smile explains the misunderstanding

an old woman carries
the corpse of a canary
(all the animals died a little earlier)
he was so nice – she says weeping
he understood everything
and when I said to him –
her voice is lost in the general noise

even a lumberjack
whom one would never suspect of such things
an old bowed fellow
catches to his breast an axe
– all my life she was mine
she will be mine here too
she nourished me there

she will nourish me here
nobody has the right
– he says –
I won't give her up

those who as it seems
have obeyed the orders without pain
go lowering their heads as a sign of consent
but in their clenched fists they hide
fragments of letters ribbons clippings of hair
and photographs
which they naïvely think
won't be taken from them

so they appear
a moment before
the final division
of those gnashing their teeth
from those singing psalms

Apollo and Marsyas

THE real duel of Apollo
with Marsyas
(absolute ear
versus immense range)
takes place in the evening
when as we already know
the judges
have awarded victory to the god

bound tight to a tree
meticulously stripped of his skin
Marsyas

APOLLO AND MARSYAS

howls
before the howl reaches his tall ears
he reposes in the shadow of that howl

shaken by a shudder of disgust
Apollo is cleaning his instrument

only seemingly
is the voice of Marsyas
monotonous
and composed of a single-vowel
Aaa

in reality
Marsyas relates
the inexhaustible wealth
of his body

bald mountains of liver
white ravines of aliment
rustling forests of lung
sweet hillocks of muscle
joints bile blood and shudders
the wintry wind of bone
over the salt of memory
shaken by a shudder of disgust
Apollo is cleaning his instrument

now to the chorus
is joined the backbone of Marsyas
in principle the same A
only deeper with the addition of rust

this is already beyond the endurance
of the god with nerves of artificial fibre

along a gravel path
hedged with box
the victor departs
wondering
whether out of Marsyas' howling
there will not some day arise
a new kind
of art – let us say – concrete

suddenly
at his feet
falls a petrified nightingale

he looks back
and sees
that the hair of the tree to which Marsyas was
      fastened
is white
completely

The Rain

WHEN my older brother
came back from war
he had on his forehead a little silver star
and under the star
an abyss

a splinter of shrapnel
hit him at Verdun
or perhaps at Grünwald
(he'd forgotten the details)

he used to talk much
in many languages
but he liked most of all
the language of history

until losing breath
he commanded his dead pals to run
Roland Kowalski Hannibal

he shouted
that this was the last crusade
that Carthage soon would fall
and then sobbing confessed
that Napoleon did not like him

we looked at him
getting paler and paler
abandoned by his senses
he turned slowly into a monument

into musical shells of ears
entered a stone forest
and the skin of his face
was secured
with the blind dry
buttons of eyes

nothing was left him
but touch

what stories
he told with his hands
in the right he had romances
in the left soldier's memories

they took my brother
and carried him out of town
he returns every fall
slim and very quiet
(he does not want to come in)
he knocks at the window for me

we walk together in the streets
and he recites to me
improbable tales
touching my face
with blind fingers of rain

Jonah

Now the Lord had prepared a great fish to swallow up Jonah

JONAH son of Amittai
running away from a dangerous mission
boarded a ship sailing
from Joppa to Tarshish

JONAH

the well-known things happened
great wind tempest
the crew casts Jonah forth into the deep
the sea ceases from her raging
the foreseen fish comes swimming up
three days and three nights
Jonah prays in the fish's belly
which vomits him out at last
on dry land

the modern Jonah
goes down like a stone
if he comes across a whale
he hasn't time even to gasp

saved
he behaves more cleverly
than his biblical colleague
the second time he does not take on
a dangerous mission
he grows a beard
and far from the sea
far from Nineveh
under an assumed name
deals in cattle and antiques
agents of Leviathan
can be bought
they have no sense of fate
they are the functionaries of chance

in a neat hospital
Jonah dies of cancer
himself not knowing very well
who he really was

the parable
applied to his head
expires
and the balm of the legend
does not take to his flesh

Our Fear

OUR fear
does not wear a night shirt
does not have owl's eyes
does not lift a casket lid
does not extinguish a candle

does not have a dead man's face either

our fear
is a scrap of paper
found in a pocket
'warn Wójcik
the place on Długa Street is hot'

our fear
does not rise on the wings of the tempest
does not sit on a church tower
it is down-to-earth

it has the shape
of a bundle made in haste
with warm clothing
provisions
and arms

our fear
does not have the face of a dead man
the dead are gentle to us
we carry them on our shoulders
sleep under the same blanket
close their eyes
adjust their lips
pick a dry spot
and bury them

not too deep
not too shallow

The Pebble

THE pebble
is a perfect creature

equal to itself
mindful of its limits

filled exactly
with a pebbly meaning

with a scent which does not remind one of anything
does not frighten anything away does not arouse desire

its ardour and coldness
are just and full of dignity

I feel a heavy remorse
when I hold it in my hand
and its noble body
is permeated by false warmth

– Pebbles cannot be tamed
to the end they will look at us
with a calm and very clear eye

Revelation

Two perhaps three
times
I was sure
I would touch the essence
and would know

REVELATION

the web of my formula
made of allusions as in the Phaedo
had also the rigour
of Heisenberg's equation

I was sitting immobile
with watery eyes
I felt my backbone
fill with quiet certitude

earth stood still
heaven stood still
my immobility
was nearly perfect

the postman rang
I had to pour out the dirty water
prepare tea

Siva lifted his finger
the furniture of heaven and earth
started to spin again

I returned to my room
where is that perfect peace
the idea of a glass
was being spilled all over the table

I sat down immobile
with watery eyes
filled with emptiness
i.e. with desire

If it happens to me once more
I shall be moved neither by the postman's bell
nor by the shouting of angels

I shall sit
immobile
my eyes fixed
upon the heart of things

a dead star

a black drop of infinity

Study of the Object

I

THE most beautiful is the object
which does not exist

it does not serve to carry water
or to preserve the ashes of a hero

it was not cradled by Antigone
nor was a rat drowned in it

it has no hole
and is entirely open

STUDY OF THE OBJECT

seen
from every side
which means
hardly anticipated

the hairs
of all its lines
join
in one stream of light

neither
blindness
nor
death
can take away the object
which does not exist

2

mark the place
where stood the object
which does not exist
with a black square
it will be
a simple dirge
for the beautiful absence

manly regret
imprisoned
in a quadrangle

3

now
all space
swells like an ocean

a hurricane beats
on the black sail

the wing of a blizzard circles
over the black square

and the island sinks
beneath the salty increase

4

now you have
empty space
more beautiful than the object

more beautiful than the place it leaves
it is the pre-world
a white paradise
of all possibilities
you may enter there
cry out
vertical-horizontal

perpendicular lightning
strikes the naked horizon

we can stop at that
anyway you have already created a world

5

obey the counsels
of the inner eye

do not yield
to murmurs mutterings smackings

it is the uncreated world
crowding before the gates of your canvas

angels are offering
the rosy wadding of clouds

trees are inserting everywhere
slovenly green hair

kings are praising purple
and commanding their trumpeters
to gild

even the whale asks for a portrait

obey the counsels of the inner eye
admit no one

6

extract
from the shadow of the object
which does not exist
from polar space
from the stern reveries of the inner eye
a chair

beautiful and useless
like a cathedral in the wilderness

place on the chair
a crumpled tablecloth
add to the idea of order
the idea of adventure

let it be a confession of faith
before the vertical struggling with the horizontal

let it be
quieter than angels
prouder than kings
more substantial than a whale
let it have the face of the last things

we ask reveal o chair
the depths of the inner eye
the iris of necessity
the pupil of death

A Naked Town

ON the plain that town flat like an iron sheet
with mutilated hand of its cathedral a pointing claw
with pavements the colour of intestines houses stripped
    of their skin

the town beneath a yellow wave of sun
a chalky wave of moon

o town what a town tell me what's the name of that
    town
under what star on what road

about people: they work at the slaughter-house in an
    immense building
of raw concrete blocks around them the odour of blood
and the penitential psalm of animals Are there poets there
    (silent poets)
there are troops a big rattle of barracks on the outskirts
on Sunday beyond the bridge in prickly bushes on cold
    sand on rusty grass girls receive soldiers
there are as well some places dedicated to dreams The
    cinema
with a white wall on which splash the shadows of the
    absent
little halls where alcohol is poured into glass thin and
    thick
there are also dogs at last hungry dogs that howl
and in that fashion indicate the borders of the town Amen

so you still ask what's the name of that town
which deserves biting anger where is that town
on the cords of what winds beneath what column of air
and who lives there people with the same skin as ours
or people with our faces or

ZBIGNIEW HERBERT

The Fathers of a Star

CLOCKS were running as usual so they waited only
for the avalanche effect and whether it would follow
the curve traced on a sheet of ether
they were calm and certain on the tower of their calcu-
     lations
amid gentle volcanoes under the guard of lead
they were covered by glass and silence and a sky without
     secrets
clocks were running as usual so the explosion came

with their hats pulled tightly over their brows they
     walked away
smaller than their clothes the fathers of a star
they thought about a kite from childhood the tense
     string trembled in their hands
and now everything was separated from them
clocks worked for them they were left only
like an heirloom from father an old silver pulse

in the evening in a house near a forest without animals or
     ferns
with a concrete path and an electric owl
they will read the tale of Daedalus to their children
the Greek was right he didn't want the moon or the stars
he was only a bird he remained in the order of nature
and the things he created followed him like animals
like a cloak he wore on his shoulders his wings and his
     fate

Elegy of Fortinbras
for C. M.

Now that we're alone we can talk prince man to man
though you lie on the stairs and see no more than a dead
    ant
nothing but black sun with broken rays
I could never think of your hands without smiling
and now that they lie on the stone like fallen nests
they are as defenceless as before The end is exactly this
The hands lie apart The sword lies apart The head apart
and the knight's feet in soft slippers

You will have a soldier's funeral without having been
    a soldier
the only ritual I am acquainted with a little
There will be no candles no singing only cannon-fuses
    and bursts
crepe dragged on the pavement helmets boots artillery
    horses drums drums I know nothing exquisite
those will be my manoeuvres before I start to rule
one has to take the city by the neck and shake it a bit

Anyhow you had to perish Hamlet you were not for life
you believed in crystal notions not in human clay
always twitching as if asleep you hunted chimeras
wolfishly you crunched the air only to vomit
you knew no human thing you did not know even how
    to breathe

Now you have peace Hamlet you accomplished what you
    had to
and you have peace The rest is not silence but belongs to
    me
you chose the easier part an elegant thrust
but what is heroic death compared with eternal watching
with a cold apple in one's hand on a narrow chair
with a view of the ant-hill and the clock's dial

Adieu prince I have tasks a sewer project
and a decree on prostitutes and beggars
I must also elaborate a better system of prisons
since as you justly said Denmark is a prison
I go to my affairs This night is born
a star named Hamlet We shall never meet
what I shall leave will not be worth a tragedy

It is not for us to greet each other or bid farewell we live
    on archipelagos
and that water these words what can they do what can
    they do prince

The Return of the Proconsul

I'VE decided to return to the emperor's court
once more I shall see if it's possible to live there
I could stay here in this remote province
under the full sweet leaves of the sycamore
and the gentle rule of sickly nepotists

THE RETURN OF THE PROCONSUL

when I return I don't intend to commend myself
I shall applaud in measured portions
smile in ounces frown discreetly
for that they will not give me a golden chain
this iron one will suffice

I've decided to return tomorrow or the day after
I cannot live among vineyards nothing here is mine
trees have no roots houses no foundations the rain is
      glassy flowers smell of wax
a dry cloud rattles against the empty sky
so I shall return tomorrow or the day after in any case
      I shall return

I must come to terms with my face again
with my lower lip so it knows how to curb scorn
with my eyes so they remain ideally empty
and with that miserable chin the hare of my face
which trembles when the chief of guards walks in

of one thing I am sure I will not drink wine with him
when he brings his goblet nearer I will lower my eyes
and pretend I'm picking bits of food from between my
      teeth
besides the emperor likes courage of convictions
to a certain extent to a certain reasonable extent
he is after all a man like everyone else
and already tired by all those tricks with poison
he cannot drink his fill incessant chess
this left cup is for Drusus from the right one pretend to
      sip

then drink only water never lose sight of Tacitus
take a walk in the garden and return when the corpse has
    been removed

I've decided to return to the emperor's court
yes I hope that things will work out somehow

A Halt

WE halted in a town the host
ordered the table to be moved to the garden the first star
shone out and faded we were breaking bread
crickets were heard in the evening weeds
a cry but a cry of a child otherwise the bustle
of insects of men a thick scent of earth
those who were sitting with their backs to the wall
saw the gallows hill now a violet hill
on the wall the dense ivy of executions

we were eating a lot
as is usual when no one must pay

A Wooden Die

A WOODEN die can be described only from without. We
are therefore condemned to eternal ignorance of its
essence. Even if it is quickly cut in two, immediately its

inside becomes a wall and there occurs the lightning-swift transformation of a mystery into a skin.

For this reason it is impossible to lay foundations for the psychology of a stone ball, of an iron bar, of a wooden cube.

The Tongue

INADVERTENTLY I passed the border of her teeth and swallowed her agile tongue. It lives inside me now, like a Japanese fish. It brushes against my heart and my diaphragm as if against the walls of an aquarium. It stirs silt from the bottom.

She whom I deprived of a voice stares at me with big eyes and waits for a word.

Yet I do not know which tongue to use when speaking to her – the stolen one or the one which melts in my mouth from an excess of heavy goodness.

From Mythology

FIRST there was a god of night and tempest, a black idol without eyes, before whom they leaped, naked and smeared with blood. Later on, in the times of the republic, there were many gods with wives, children, creaking beds, and harmlessly exploding thunderbolts. At the end only superstitious neurotics carried in their pockets little statues of salt, representing the god of irony. There was no greater god at that time.

Then came the barbarians. They too valued highly the little god of irony. They would crush it under their heels and add it to their dishes.

The End of a Dynasty

THE whole royal family was living in one room at that time. Outside the windows was a wall, and under the wall, a dump. There, rats used to bite cats to death. This was not seen. The windows had been painted over with lime.

When the executioners came, they found an everyday scene.

His Majesty was improving the regulations of the Holy Trinity regiment, the occultist Philippe was trying to soothe the Queen's nerves by suggestion, the Crown Prince, rolled into a ball, was sleeping in an armchair, and the Grand (and skinny) Duchesses were singing pious songs and mending linen.

As for the valet, he stood against a partition and tried to imitate the tapestry.

The Emperor's Dream

A CREVICE! shouts the Emperor in his sleep, and the canopy of ostrich plumes trembles. The soldiers who pace the corridors with unsheathed swords believe the Emperor dreams about a siege. Just now he saw a fissure in the wall and wants them to break into the fortress.

In fact the Emperor is now a wood-louse who scurries across the floor, seeking remnants of food. Suddenly he sees overhead an immense foot about to crush him. The Emperor hunts for a crevice in which to squeeze. The floor is smooth and slippery.

Yes. Nothing is more ordinary than the dreams of Emperors.

The Envoy of Mr. Cogito

Go where those others went to the dark boundary
for the golden fleece of nothingness your last prize

go upright among those who are on their knees
among those with their backs turned and those
      toppled in the dust

you were saved not in order to live
you have little time you must give testimony

be courageous when the mind deceives you be
      courageous
in the final account only this is important

and let your helpless Anger be like the sea
whenever you hear the voice of the insulted and
      beaten

let your sister Scorn not leave you
for the informers executioners cowards—they will win
they will go to your funeral and with relief will
      throw a lump of earth

the woodborer will write your smoothed-over
    biography

and do not forgive truly it is not in your power
to forgive in the name of those betrayed at dawn

beware however of unnecessary pride
keep looking at your clown's face in the mirror
repeat: I was called—weren't there better ones than I

beware of dryness of heart love the morning spring
the bird with an unknown name the winter oak

light on a wall the splendor of the sky
they don't need your warm breath
they are there to say: no one will console you

be vigilant—when the light on the mountains gives
    the sign—arise and go
as long as blood turns in the breast your dark star

repeat old incantations of humanity fables and legends
because this is how you will attain the good you will
    not attain
repeat great words repeat them stubbornly
like those crossing the desert who perished in the sand

and they will reward you with what they have at
    hand
with the whip of laughter with murder on a garbage
    heap

go because only in this way will you be admitted to
    the company of cold skulls
to the company of your ancestors: Gilgamesh Hector
    Roland
the defenders of the kingdom without limit and the
    city of ashes

Be faithful Go

Translated by Bogdana and John Carpenter

TADEUSZ NOWAK
(born 1930)

NOWAK's peasant background offers the indispensable commentary to his poems. Mass migration from the villages to the cities has been a major fact since the end of World War II, but for few poets has this become a personal problem. Yet to feel alien in new surroundings and to know that one would be even more of a stranger if one returned to one's native village can be a serious problem – which it is for Nowak. He has been called a 'peasant surrealist'. His poetry is elaborate yet a tangle of images which are nearly always related to the first perceptions of a peasant child. The richness of the words referring to agricultural labours, tools, harnesses, folkloric tales and songs, the metaphorical construction of sentences bound by rhymes – do not invite translation of his poems as it would mean losing their freshness and originality. I could not resist the temptation of trying my hand at one, relatively simple, a glimpse of his lost kingdom.

I Leave Myself

I LEAVE myself – salt leaves the sea
and iron seeps from the stem of silence.
All the dogs of the world follow my musk
on a threshhold, in forest hay and in the wrist of a river.

And I am not. There is only a raspberry bush
beside which peasants carry pianos.
And they pluck at me, like a parson at his rosary
when he stares into the purple of the bishop's orchard.

And I see from afar the dream's blue haystack
and around it the laddered mouths of horses
to whom my grandfather, their god, is handing sugar
when leaning from the cradle of my childhood heaven.

BOGDAN CZAYKOWSKI
(born 1932)

CZAYKOWSKI was seven when he left Poland, deported with his family to northern Russia. After many wanderings through Persia and Africa, he reached England where he grew up, studied at the University of London and obtained his M.A. in Slavic Literatures. His fate was far from unique: in London he joined a group of beginning writers whose biographies and situation were similar to his own. They went through English schools and, though perfectly bilingual, chose to write in Polish. In revolt against the older generation of the emigrés, separated from the public in Poland by the division of Europe, they have succeeded nevertheless in editing a little magazine and in publishing their volumes of poems. Their development as poets parallels, in many respects, the transformations taking place in their country of origin. Contrary to some elder emigré poets who remained faithful to the verse of *Skamander*, they rejected metre and rhyme. The cordial relations they have been maintaining with their colleagues in Poland since the liberalization of 1956 testify to a similarity of views and a mutual respect. Czaykowski is perhaps the most outspoken among them in that he attacks directly the pitiful condition of the poet in exile and applies in that way the old principle of existential wisdom: to transform, through awareness, one's weakness into material and, thence, into the source of one's energy. For many years he has been teaching Polish literature at the University of British Columbia, Vancouver.

BOGDAN CZAYKOWSKI

A Prayer

Throw me into a cloud o lord

but do not make me a drop of rain
I do not want to return to earth

throw me into a flower o lord

but do not make me a bee
I would die from an excess of industrious sweetness

throw me into a lake

but do not make me a fish o lord
I would not be able to become cold-blooded

throw me into a forest
like a pine cone on the grass
let no red-haired squirrels find me

throw me into a calm shape of a stone
but not on the pavement of a London street
o lord I worry and bite walls in this alien city

you who turn me over fire
pluck me from flames
and deposit me on a quiet white cloud

A Revolt in Verse

I WAS born there.
I did not choose the place.
Why was I not born simply in the grass.
Grass grows everywhere.
Only deserts would not accept me.
Or I could have been born in a skein of the wind
When the air is breathing.
But I was born there.
They chained me when I was a baby
And they put me into the world with my little chains.
I am here. I was born there.
Had I at least been born at sea.
You, magnetic iron
Which turn me constantly towards a pole,
You are heavy; without you I am so light
That I lose the perception of my weight.
So I bear those little chains
And I toss them as a lion tosses his mane.
People from over there shout:
Come back.
They call me: chip, chip, chip
Millet and weeds are poured in vain.
Dog, into the kennel!
I am a poet (one has to have a name).
The language is my chain.
Words are my collar.
I was born there.
Why was I not born simply in the grass.

JERZY HARASYMOWICZ
(born 1933)

HARASYMOWICZ'S first volume published in 1956 bore the title *Wonders* and it defines his work quite well. His poems are surrealistic fairy tales. His is a world of murky cats swearing in slang, trees acting as princesses, saints from old paintings reciting prayers on the choir loft of an abandoned country church, kettles wearing red tailcoats, carpets with masochistic inclinations. His metaphorical inventiveness seems unlimited, and he builds his tenderly or cruelly humourous stories in verse on the sensuous qualities of the simplest things he observes. I see a basic difference between such a poet as Harasymowicz and the poets of America or France: his imagination is not urban and, consequently, he can name an astonishing number of plants, trees, birds, often playing with those names and inventing images by mixing nature with the history of art. The medieval city of Cracow, where he lives, is often present in his poems, but the woods and remote villages of the highlands are particularly close to his heart. His stubborn clinging to poetry conceived as the realm of personal myths protects him from those who ask for 'meaning' and he has always maintained a complete indifference to ratiocinations. It is a pity that the musical quality of his poetry cannot be rendered in translation.

A Green Lowland of Pianos

IN the evening
as far as the eye can see
herds
of black pianos

up to their knees
in the mire
they listen to the frogs

they gurgle in water
with chords of rapture

they are entranced
by froggish, moonish spontaneity

after the vacation
they cause scandals
in a concert hall
during the artistic milking
suddenly they lie down
like cows

looking with indifference
at the white flowers
of the audience

at the gesticulating
of the ushers

The Thistle

In the presence of thistles
don't tell me
about the stupid
red face of the rose

the thistle
a true philosopher
observes
the roads of life
wearing a mantle of dust

he creates
a magnificent decor
for pilgrimages

in the Vienna style of 1900
he made a fair career
but alas, misunderstood,
withdrew again
to dry highlands

and now
from priests conducting pilgrimages
he learned
the art of gesture

he became
the most profound of weeds

moving his shape
into dramatic
stony soils

people don't grasp
his meaning

his beauty
rapacious and luminous
he shows in darkness

angry and winged
he is the most perfect
model for modern angels

Leda and the Swan

The red swan
of a teapot
is hissing

Leda
is a wall
pin-curled
into little roses

she encircles the swan
with her weak arms

SISTER

in white clouds
of vapour
the wall
is soaring

the teapot spreads
its red plumes

and whistles –
the gods' locomotive
in a laurel wreath

Sister

I, ATTILA

my javelin
entwined with
creeping roses
for camouflage

before me
the realm of Botticelli

my darling axe
works here

among golden bodies
grown fat
on angelic bread

remains of some
portraited gentlemen
only their caps
red

sway
on my javelin

the flowers of annunciations
are devoured
by my horse

who jumps across
murdered angels
like huge
rosy flowers

out of the forests
of branches
my javelin
plucks
a cherub
as out of a nest

an angel on one knee
genuflects
him I bend
till his pate

is smashed against
the red marble
on the floor

SISTER

I order children
to take a stick and chase
his halo out of town
like a hoop

my horse
with his red breath
sets fire to the hair
of nascent Venus

and only Judith
is my dear
sister

a lily
enfolds her knife

I take her on my saddle
before me

through green silk
I feel the body

of her who cut a head off
as one would sniff at a rose

STANISŁAW GROCHOWIAK

(1934–1976)

GROCHOWIAK usually has been mentioned as one of the leaders of the 'new wave', together with Herbert, Białoszewski, and Harasymowicz. He uses metrical and free verse with equal ease and his penchant for contriving grotesque situations brings him close to a peculiar Polish brand of gallows humour, if not to literary cabaret. When around 1960 some veterans of the First Vanguard attacked the young poets for their 'turpism', i.e., their exploitation of the hideous and the macabre, Grochowiak was the main target. The hidden motives of the attack probably had something to do with a hostility toward the metaphysical interests of the young, which were evident in their mocking, revengeful treatment of socially acceptable feelings. It is difficult to tell whether those who were attacked themselves realized the seriousness of their orientation; the new frankness, in poetry, in student satirical theatres, in prose, understandable after the puritanism of the years 1949–56, was a complex phenomenon and the very style of 'existential despair' could dictate many devices. Grochowiak's meandering personality eludes definition, especially in view of the shifts in his technique and of his multi-faceted activity. The poems selected show the variety of his tempers.

The Village Cinema

HAMLET was shown at our cinema
Under the heavy bough of an apple tree,
The peasants stared
Into an abyss of melancholy.

Later on they stole across the heath,
Across brooks
To their huts
And for the first time they kissed the feet
Of their surprised womenfolk.

At evening by the river, the lads
Lay with their faces above the water
Watching how strangely, how smoothly,
The hair of stupid Ophelia flows by.

A Short Fairy Tale

WHO are those marching – such as we are – gnomes?
Those funny jokes of playful water,
Of fire and war? We are comic ciphers,
The indispensable butter of all philosophies.

Who goes there? It is us, the gnomes.
The rainbow brood of many God the Fathers,
Third persons agreeable to everything
Whom it is sheer pleasure to kill.

Here we are marching – in twos, with a song,
Some from Sunday excursions, some from prisons,
Others from the gallows, or from their mistresses,
And still others from a tooth x-ray.

And where are they marching – such as we are –
     gnomes?
Those funny jokes of playful water,
Of fire and war?
             – To the sweetly unknown
And promised land of statistics.

To a Lady

    I LIKE to drink a bitter tea
    From your tin cup, my Lady:
    I like to stroke your rat
    When it crawls to my feet.

    Either I chat with the poker
    Or scold the carbide lamp –
    Quite vulgar, that luminary,
    No addition to your court.

    A nice bit of untidiness, Lady,
    With this astronomy of wicked spiders,
    With the dungeon of your cellar
    Where, hooked helplessly, sides of bacon expire.

Oh, my worthy feudal Lady,
Your home is to my liking.
I am eternal liege to your hair,
A constant vassal of your rib.

Clean Men

I PREFER ugliness
It is closer to the blood circulation
Of words when they are x-rayed
And tormented

It moulds the richest shapes
It redeems with its soot
The walls of charnel houses
It gives the chilliness of statues
A mousey smell

There are people so cleanly scrubbed
That when they pass
Even a dog wouldn't growl
Though they are neither holy
Nor humble

Painting

Now it is fashionable among painters
To say, I did a piece
It is a nice fragment
Of a wall, or a thing cut out
Of some useless mouldy board

PAINTING

And I agree
Those are nothing but slices
Of walls broken up
By a huge crimson trumpet

And I agree
Those are fence posts
Little coffin slats
Tapestries of tombs

But within crimson walls
There lived an old man
With swollen foot

Within yellowed walls
The anger of a brunette who died a virgin
Was thrashing around

Within hospital walls ecstatically white
A man stood naked in fear of a bomb

Your painting
Apparently insensitive
With which you liked to laugh at big words

Will go down in time
As an ominous Pompeii
Whose people are silent
Like bells in the ashes

The Breasts of the Queen Are Turned out of Wood

T H E hands of the queen are smeared with grease
The ears of the queen are plugged with cotton
In the mouth of the queen gypsum dentures
The breasts of the queen are turned out of wood

And I brought here a tongue warm with wine
In my mouth rustling sparkling saliva
The breasts of the queen are turned out of wood

In the house of the queen a yellow candle withers
In the bed of the queen a water bottle grows cooler
The mirrors of the queen are covered with tarpaulins
In the glass of the queen a syringe is rusting

And I brought here a vigorous young belly
Also teeth tensed like instruments
The breasts of the queen are turned out of wood

From the hair of the queen leaves are falling
From the eyes of the queen a spider web slips down
The heart of the queen bursts with a soft fizzle
The breath of the queen yellows on the windowpane

And I brought here a dove in a basket
And a whole bunch of golden balloons
From the hair of the queen leaves are falling

When Nothing Remains

ONE day I shall seat you in splendour
There will be garments heavy as water
There will be stockings with a scent of apples
There will be hats, broadrimmed
And there will be metal

I want you naked in a dark landscape
Dense with bronzes chandeliers vases
From which let a vanilla punch steam
Into the sniffing nostrils of Great Danes

Rembrandt felt a similar need when he painted Saskia
Who departed again and again into her death
As if he wanted to retain her with the weight of grapes
To clamp her down with the light of precious chandeliers

JAROSŁAW MAREK RYMKIEWICZ
(born 1934)

RYMKIEWICZ, a poet with a clearly set programme, is pursuing a hazardous game with literary conventions. A similar travesty of traditional forms can be found earlier in Iwaszkiewicz and in some poets of the Second Vanguard; its purpose is not merely stylistic: through a reference to the verse of the seventeenth or the eighteenth century a poet strives to underline the strangeness of cultural patterns. He is, after all, part of a cultural pattern himself, placed in the flux of relativity. The very relativity of the style and beliefs of a poet enters, however, into conflict with his feeling of being unique, an individual whose existence is given only once. Thus by showing awareness of the relative character of his form, he alludes to two levels of existence, historical and personal. One article on Rymkiewicz's book of poems, *Metaphysics* (1964), affirms that his poetry is shaped by a tension between metaphysics and dialectics. The critic is probably right, even if his formulas are a little too fashionable. Whether Rymkiewicz's poetry is capable of bearing such a self-imposed burden is not certain. He is very brilliant in his ideas, but walking a tightrope limits one's freedom of movement. He has been hailed as one of the most promising young writers and is a highly competent translator of American and English poetry.

JAROSŁAW MAREK RYMKIEWICZ

Spinoza Was a Bee

WE were not here. Plato was a spider.
We were not here. Spinoza was a bee.

The bee suffices. It is here and there.
It is a July of clouds, a July of July.

The attribute of sting, the argument of sting.
So much for the bee: a central buzzing.

Spinoza the philosopher? Just a nightmare of the bee.
In the dream of a bee. A sovereign being.

A mathematical being. A buzzing cipher.
An analogy of the bee, the pure act of the bee.

Such is the fate of angels. Spinoza was a bee.
He was a predicate of the bee, the bee the subject.

There was no predicate. That was the fear of the spider.
That was the dream of the bee. There was no Spinoza.

So much says Nature. Here the bee suffices.
It is related to the sun, it is here and there.

This bee is only a cipher. A sovereign being.
A dream of Spinoza. Contradictory beings, what of
    them?

ERNEST BRYLL
(born 1935)

JUDGING by his poems from the *Non-unveiled face* (1963) Bryll's ideal is a dry, subdued, intellectual style full of allusions and innuendoes. His mask is made of metaphors invoking royal courts, parchments with seals, statues, the marble steps of palaces. It is obvious that he is principally indebted to his nineteenth-century precursor, Cyprian Norwid. His blank verse (usually alternate eleven- and thirteen-syllable lines with a caesura) is austere. Constant references to the history of Greece, the Middle Ages and the Renaissance add to a wilful obscurity. The question arises whether by shunning emotionality and choosing more and more oblique ways the young poets have not passed the point where poetry is menaced by causticity and aridity. It would be unwise to try to answer that question without taking the circumstances into account, since in Poland the trend is the result of a reaction to bureaucratic rhetoric. However, Bryll gradually evolved into a supporter of the communist establishment.

Nike

– AND such exactly she should be: whatever is super-
 fluous
has been hewed away by wind. Ailerons of wings
were long ago devoured by the sea. Why would she
 steer
her course worthy of a thunderbolt? Her hands are cut
 off
– there is no one deserving of her wreath. . . .
                                        Under her feet
(perhaps shadowed by a fold of her dress) survived
the prow of the Rhodes trireme – preserving a scent of
 tar,
of oarsmen's sweat, of well-jointed wood.
And that's quite enough. From it we write on,
How the ship in full foam, catching up with the arrows
darted to the enemy's broadside, crossed the waters of the
 Styx;
how the sound of bronze died out, how fire consumed
 the tints.
– And such exactly she should be. Washed by earth,
her breasts bereft of the warmth of nipples,
goddess of a sterile river. It is proper
that we see her as she is – without a head.
For to whom did she ever give a scrap of laurel to keep?
Victory was the beginning of defeats. Nothing but the
 rapture of the race
was left; the echo of shouts, pursuing
our ships faster than ever she did.

A Ballad of the Bayonet

FIRST they taught us earth. The Napoleonic death
was still: close the ranks, close the ranks . . . and they
   closed
as bleeding fingers – whoever had the harder
fist – would win. With shaggy bearskin caps
cannons' throats used to be extinguished. . . .
The bayonet alone
did not burn out, always useful:
you can carve initials with it on a concrete wall,
open tin cans. Its flame
not touched by any wind, is purer than prayer,
faultless as pious thought. A nobleman
among those thuds, that gutting of the earth,
those clownish leaps.
                        Then they taught us sky
– and again evolution turns back, a retreat
into the perfection of the reptiles, an armoured head,
a protective colour.
                        It alone requires us
to fight, standing. It alone orders us
to look at the enemy's faces, to sniff drops of sweat,
to kill sensing the heartbeat up to the hilt. To fall
tearing earth not yet corroded to the bone. . . .
It alone did not burn out. More faithful than God,
it reminds us that under the larval earth
and its smooth skin – against the gases – there is
a bit of warmth to be reached by the blade.

ERNEST BRYLL

Leviathan

Then, world, thou hast a pair of chaps, no more;
And throw between them all the food thou hast,
They'll grind the one the other.

Antony and Cleopatra

LET us believe – thé fangs do not quite close. And let our
        confidence
be Benedictine, introduce through the cleft
a single hair. This is enough. We must draw from it
constructions as clever as Jonah's psalmody
– he titillated Leviathan's tongue, he used to open its
        jaws
by praising the delights of yawning, he cheated its belly
bluffing it into satiety.
                            Still more. Taking its palate
for a firmament, as he did, let us manage
our affairs industriously, as if not even a cloud
were hanging over us. Cupidity
is here valiance. Let not the shadow
of a mouse nourish itself with crumbs from our tables.
After all we have already built our houses here. Having
        adorned
its teeth with ivy of exquisite ornaments, we change them
into venerable columns. Before long in its mouth
our temples will stand.
Then, world, thou hast a pair of chaps. Let Grace
be found even in the closing of the fangs. From the raging
        sea
they protect the landscape
ripening sweetly in the valleys of the tongue.

178

URSZULA KOZIOŁ
(born 1931)

URSZULA KOZIOŁ has published several books of poems, teaches Polish literature at a college, and lives in Wrocław, Silesia. Now when, after a complete liberation of verse from inherited patterns, Polish poets are searching for a new tie with tradition, perhaps she is right in going directly to its roots in ancient Greek poetry. This could be merely a literary exercise, but a hieratical form is for her a means of controlling violent emotion. Her 'Alarum' is a chorus: a collective memory, not her personal memory, dictates the words, as she belongs to a generation which has only a vague recollection of World War II.

Alarum

GRIEF
o grief
grief for ever

Give me the right to sorrow. Let other women
stand guard their hearths, let them be brightened by the
     light of their homes
but to me leave my tear
I shall keep safe the lament for the never-lamented.

Let maidens with armfuls of flowers go bowing to
     propitious
winds. A wedding retinue of time, let them go steeply
     and in crowds
and lift the harvest overhead in lofty greeting,

while it is for me to say farewell. For many of the brave
     did perish,
not all of them full-grown, but always
in thirst for light. And from them
their light escaped before the sun went down.

And Antigone did not come to bury her unburied
     brothers.
One of her, turned into smoke
or perhaps into a shadow on a stone –
another, no more than her own gesture or readiness, all
     overtaken by smoke,
shadow. So the bracket of her hands remains open
and the unaccomplished design of the act hovers.

ALARUM

And thus to weep for her too, and –
great is the number of the unknown. The undivided
tears are left to be apportioned.

Someone must be a drainpipe of tears for the un-
lamented.
For there is never enough regret, never enough memory.
The women of old knew it.
Mournfully dragging their hair on the ground or wren-
ching their fingers they raised alarum
and knocking their rattles performed their duty.

And yet in death – till now – there is nothing,
in death till now there is nothing but grief.

STANISŁAW BARAŃCZAK
(born 1946)

WITH Stanisław Barańczak we enter a new phase in Polish post-war literary life. He is quite representative of a generation who strongly reacted to a dreary, though no more than half-heartedly totalitarian, system maintained by the omnipresent Security Police. In the nineteen seventies, especially after a brutal suppression of university student protests in 1968, the 'anti-zionist' campaign of the government, and police shootings at workers in the Gdańsk area in 1970, young poets turned a 'linguistic' brand of poetry into a political weapon by taking apart the official language of the mass media. The whole decade of 1970–80 was marked by the appearance of independent publishing ventures, with the number of uncensored periodicals and books constantly growing. Barańczak, along with many of his colleagues, was blacklisted and could be printed only in those 'samizdat' publications. Offered a professorship at Harvard (by profession he is a literary scholar and taught at the University of Poznań), he had to wait a couple of years for his passport. In the fall of 1981 he began to teach Polish literature at Harvard. He is an excellent translator from English (English metaphysical poets) and from Russian (Osip Mandelstam, Josif Brodsky). His own poetry has been, at least until now, preeminently political.

STANISŁAW BARAŃCZAK

If You Have to Scream, Please *Do It Quietly*

IF you have to scream, *please* do it quietly (the walls
have
ears), if you have to make love,

please turn out the lights (a neighbor
has
binoculars), if you have

to live here, *please* don't bar the door (the authorities
have
right of entry), if you

have to suffer, *please* do it in your own home (life
has
its laws), if

you have to live, *please* limit yourself in everything
      (everything
has
a limit)

                              Translated by Frank Kujawinski

The Humane Conditions

THE humane conditions of life, which are guaranteed
me: the right to human feelings,
to uncertainty, to fear, to (how very human it is)

184

hatred (obviously toward enemies who are
carefully selected for me so that I needn't bother);
the right to human (no cause for shame)
physiology: to sweating (at work), to weeping
(into the pillow), to bleeding even (at
the bloodbank); I have not only the right
but also the duty to display all the
human weaknesses: no one, for instance, compels me
to be a hero, i.e., to speak the truth,
not to inform, to refrain from very human
need of kicking a man when he's down; nothing
that's human is alien to me, and also
nothing that's alien is human to me, we live
here, within our own circle, we need no aliens,
we are all good pals, regular guys,
just people.

Translated by Magnus Jan Krynski
and Robert A. Maguire

Never Really

I never really felt the cold, never
was devoured by lice, never knew
true hunger, humiliation, fear for my life:

at times I wonder whether I have any right to write

Translated by Magnus Jan Krynski
and Robert A. Maguire

STANISŁAW BARAŃCZAK

Those Men, So Powerful

THOSE men, so powerful, always shown
somewhat from below by crouching cameramen,
    who lift
a heavy foot to crush me, no, to climb
the steps of the plane, who raise a hand
to strike me, no, to greet the crowds
obediently waving little flags, those men who sign
my death warrant, no, just a trade
agreement which is promptly dried by a servile
    blotter,

those men so brave, with upraised foreheads
standing in an open car, who
so courageously visit the battleline of harvest
    operations,
step into a furrow as though entering a trench,
those men with hard hands capable of banging
the rostrum and slapping the backs
of people bowed in obeisance who have just this
    moment been pinned
to their best suits with a medal,

always
you were so afraid of them,
you were so small
compared to them, who always stood above
you, on steps, rostrums, platforms,
and yet it is enough for just one instant to stop
being afraid a little less,

186

to become convinced that they are the ones,
that they are the ones who are most afraid.

Translated by Magnus Jan Krynski
and Robert A. Maguire

If Porcelain, Then Only the Kind

IF porcelain, then only the kind
you won't miss under the shoe of a mover or the
    tread of a tank;
if a chair, then one not too comfortable, lest
there be regret in getting up and leaving;
if clothing, then just so much as can fit in a suitcase,
if books, then those which can be carried in the
    memory,
if plans, then those which can be overlooked
when the time comes for the next move
to another street, continent, historical period
or world:

who told you that you were permitted to settle in?
who told you that this or that would last forever?
did no one ever tell you that you will never
in the world
feel at home in the world.

Translated by Frank Kujawinski

ADAM ZAGAJEWSKI
(born 1945)

A poet and literary critic, Zagajewski says in his poems things unthinkable a few years ago and in that way illustrates a radical change that occurred in the minds of the youngest generation of poets. With the last vestiges of the communist doctrine discredited, what remains, in fact, is the phenomenon of a naked force using the doctrine as a smoke screen. Zagajewski and his contemporaries write in a plain, simple language and express in it the most obvious truths, which they had not been able to learn at school. They discuss without inhibition sad facts in the recent history of their country reduced as it is to the role of a rebellious prisoner. Thus it seems that Polish poetry, after having assimilated several avant-garde movements, is now primarily occupied with restoring a sense of civic responsibility.

ADAM ZAGAJEWSKI

Freedom

WHAT is freedom? ask the philosophers.
I, too, wonder; at one time I maintain
that it means guaranteed liberty
in the face of the power of the State, or else
I emphasize that it is the strength of convictions,
the sovereignty of spirit
and the loyalty to one's own vocation.
But even when I am at a loss to define
the essence of freedom
I know full well the meaning
of captivity.

Translated by Antony Graham

I Talked to a Frenchman

THE meaning of the word: independent country—
need not amount to much.
A clear Sunday afternoon, from the windows
comes the music of conversations,
the sounds of Chopin.
On Friday at daybreak
you hear the hard knock of a hammer,
a swear word and the mocking banter
of the working men. An independent country
does not mean a great deal.
No more than a fountainhead of water
in a stony valley among the rocks.

Translated by Antony Graham

Verses About Poland

I read verses about Poland
written by foreign poets. Germans and Russians
have not only rifles, but also
ink, pens, a little heart and a lot
of imagination. Poland—in their verses—
resembles a reckless unicorn
feeding on the wool of tapestries,
it is beautiful, weak and imprudent.
I do not comprehend the working
of the mechanism of illusion
but even I, a sober reader,
am enchanted by that legendary, defenseless country
on which feed black eagles, hungry emperors,
the Third Reich and the Third Rome.

Translated by Antony Graham